IT'S TIME FOR THE MOTIVATOR!

40 ACHIEVEMENT PRINCIPLES FOR MAXIMIZING YOUR FULL POTENTIAL

Quinn M. Gentry, PhD/MBA

Leadership and Entrepreneur Life Coach

Messages of Empowerment Productions, LLC: Atlanta, Georgia

ISBN: 978-0-9968167-2-4

MESSAGES OF EMPOWERMENT
Productions, LLC

Book Cover Designer: Elaine Young, Hopscotch Communications
Project Editors: William C. Jones, Eric "Bo" Foston, and Gwen Julien

Printed and Published in the United States of America

DEDICATION

This book is dedicated to my motivators who inspired me to pen my perspectives on maximizing one's full potential under less than perfect conditions.

"After you've done all you can, STAND! You may be standing alone, but the good news is you are still standing! If you can stand, you can walk. If you can walk, you can run, and if you can run, you can mount up on wings and SOAR! Because I believe if you put your mind to it, you can do it!"

Now Let's Go!

Dr. Quinn Motivates

CONTENTS

"THE **40** ACHIEVEMENT PRINCIPLES"

About the Author

Quinn M. Gentry, PhD, MBA

quinn.gentry@team-moe.com | www.team-moe.com

President & CEO | Social & Behavioral Scientist | Executive Coach | Author
Speaker | Spoken word artist | Playwright

Dr. Quinn M. Gentry (affectionately known as "Dr. Quinn") is President and CEO of Messages of Empowerment Productions, LLC (TEAM-MOE) – a public health and management consulting company located in Atlanta, GA that specializes in organizational effectiveness, women's health, program evaluation, and community engagement. Prior to launching her own business, Dr. Quinn worked as a corporate executive for several Fortune 500 companies, including Johnson & Johnson, Kimberly-Clark, and Wal-Mart corporations. She also served as a Political Intelligence Officer at the Central Intelligence Agency (CIA) and later held behavioral research and teaching positions at Emory University and Georgia State University.

Dr. Quinn's more than 25 years of leadership experience in government, corporate, and non-profit organizations contribute to her being highly respected and a sought-after workshop facilitator, consultant, and public speaker. Her prior leadership and officer positions held include: Technical Leader and Program Director for multiple sponsored research projects; President of the *Black Affairs Program* for the CIA; and she served seven years as Chair of the *Leadership Summit* for the National Coalition of 100 Black Women Inc. - Metropolitan Atlanta Chapter. In addition, Dr. Quinn is a former Program Director for the 100 Black Men's (The Atlanta Chapter) Project Success Mentoring Program and Founder and Managing Director of The Inner-City Achievers Foundation. Other select professional accolades include – past recipient of the Texas Christian University (TCU) Leadership Award, valedictorian of the 2013 Small Business Administration's (SBA) Emerging Leaders Program, recipient of the Red Pump Award for her work in HIV Prevention and Intervention, and the recipient of the Center for Black Women's Wellness 20th Anniversary Health Leader Award.

Dr. Quinn is known primarily for her work as a social and behavioral scientist and subject matter expert (SME) on a wide range of social issues and health threats affecting women and girls. She has also served as a Principal Investigator, Senior Scientist, and Research Analyst on numerous assessment and evaluation studies at the federal, state, and local government levels. As an executive leadership coach, Dr. Quinn has conducted workshops and customized sessions for business and community leaders, managers, frontline, and technical staff, as well as for entrepreneurs and the faith-based community.

She has authored over 50 publications and presented at top-tier professional conferences in the fields of public and women's health, HIV/AIDS, and sociology. She wrote, directed, and produced "Divine Intervention," a series of monologue readings to bring awareness to the intersection of HIV, mental illness, substance abuse, domestic violence, and homelessness among black women. Dr. Quinn has also authored 11 books on a broad range of topics, namely leadership, entrepreneurship, program evaluation, mentoring, and black feminism. She currently has a number of manuscripts underway in her quest to publish 50 books by age 50!

Dr. Quinn completed a post-doctoral fellowship at the Johns Hopkins University Bloomberg School of Public Health and holds a Ph.D. degree in Sociology from Georgia State University. She earned an M.B.A. degree in Marketing from Clark Atlanta University and completed her undergraduate studies at Texas Christian University where she received a B.A. degree with dual majors in Political Science and History, and a minor in International Relations. Dr. Quinn is a licensed minister and graduate of the Women's Institute of Ministry, and has served as a course instructor for the Bible Institute at Elizabeth Baptist Church in Atlanta, GA. She is a native of Atlanta where she grew up in the inner-city's Perry Homes Community. She is a proud and active member of Alpha Kappa Alpha Sorority, Inc. and enjoys dancing, listening to live bands, the spoken word, and creative writing.

ABOUT MESSAGES OF EMPOWERMENT PRODUCTIONS, LLC

Messages of Empowerment Productions, LLC (TEAM-MOE) is a management consulting firm specializing in public health, new program development, organization effectiveness, and knowledge dissemination. Headquartered in Atlanta, Ga., TEAM-MOE achieves its business objectives through an extensive national network of dedicated subject matter experts and small consulting firms.

Our Mission
TEAM-MOE contributes to the process of changing: **(1)** individual lives, **(2)** organizations, **(3)** communities, **(4)** systems, and **(5)** structures in a way that enhances social and health opportunities for vulnerable populations.

Our Vision
TEAM-MOE accomplishes its mission by: Evaluating Programs * Educating Providers * Empowering People * Engaging the Public

Our Four (4) Practice Areas
TEAM-MOE is organized into four (4) main practice areas: (1) Program Evaluation; (2) Organizational Effectiveness; (3) Social and Behavioral Intervention; and (4) Community Engagement and Knowledge Dissemination.

Subject Matter Expertise
TEAM-MOE's staff and affiliates have expertise in the following subject matter areas: Adolescent Girls Development * Business, Brand Management, and Entrepreneurship * Child Welfare and Juvenile Justice * Faith-based Programs and Interventions * HIV/AIDS/STDs Awareness, Monitoring and Management * Homelessness and Supportive Housing * Leadership Development * Maternal and Child Health * Mentoring and After-school Programs * Organizational Capacity and Effectiveness * Social and Structural Determinants of Health * Substance Abuse and Mental Health Treatment and Aftercare * Teen Pregnancy Prevention and Intervention Treatment Court and Supportive Services * Violence against Women * Women and Girls Health

Foreword by Becky A. Davis

I wasn't surprised when I heard that Quinn was writing a book with the idea of helping people through motivation to be high achievers and maximize their creative thinking. I met her in 2012, and since that time, have admired her for her work ethic, her love of knowledge, love of life, ability to motivate people and make them smile. I have also been personally inspired by her life's story, so I was touched and honored when she asked me to write the forward for this book.

I've had a pretty successful career and life by most measures, but there is still many a day when I get out of bed in the morning and feel like I am not sure I am up to the task. I have this doubt that creeps into my thoughts that says, "Maybe you are not as good as you think you are or maybe I need to get more education." I know that most people have felt similar thoughts and feelings before but we keep them to ourselves and hope they just fade away. That's why I am so excited about this book and it's why I think it is important to look at how we think, look at our past, our relationships, and do the work needed to change our lives.

I've worked the last 25 years leading people and teams and I am convinced that every person has issues and life circumstances that must be addressed to really unleash a new life. You will not flourish personally or professionally if you do not "do your work" on yourself. Yes, you can get ahead but you will always have a set-back in the same area of life until you deal with it and "touch" the wound.

I finally touched my wound. My parents divorced when I was two years old. My father got married pretty soon after the divorce. There were four of us kids and we would spend the weekends with my dad but my step-mom, who always had something negative to say about my mom when we would visit, sometimes seemed to interfere with my relationship with my father. When I was 15, my dad moved away to another city and did not tell his kids, or my mom, that he'd moved. The way I found out was, the summer was quickly approaching and I called his house and the telephone number was not in service. So I called my grandfather, his dad, to tell him to have my dad call me because I was coming for the summer. My grandfather informed me that my dad had moved from Dallas to Houston, Texas a month ago. Our relationship started going downhill faster at that point. My step-mom had two kids with my father and that's where she wanted my father's time to be spent and not with us. It always felt like we were a burden when we came to visit our dad.

I went to college and my sophomore year in school I called to ask my dad for $20 to buy food until I got paid at the end of the month. $20 went a long way 25 years ago. It was my first time calling to ask him for anything since I was in elementary school. He said he would send it. Well, it never came and that was the straw that broke my heart. I was angry with him for years. I tell you this story because the content in this book reveals the work that I had to do to truly move forward in life and in my relationship with my father. The reconciliation chapter reflects the stages that I had to move through in order to heal myself. As an adult, I had to face reality that he was just trying to please his wife to have a happy home. I had to move the negative **emotions** out of my thoughts then call a **ceasefire**. I was **open** to a new relationship as an adult so we created a **new deal**. I let go of my bruised ego because I wanted a relationship with my father. This was the beginning of transformation for our relationship.

Quinn helps you to discover the hidden and locked away thoughts that are stopping or slowing you down from a fulfilling life and total happiness. You will be inspired, understand the power of reconciliations, identify life's confirmations, transform who you are, then live in a state of motivation, which describes the current relationship I have with my father. I'm motivated to do the work and be intentional about building a healthy relationship with him. To date I have the best relationship I have ever had with my dad but it's because I did my work. Everything you read in this book is about doing your inner work. Learning from life's lessons and putting new behaviors in place is what success is all about. And it is something you can learn to do. This great book is going to help a whole lot of people learn to be successful holistically.

Becky A. Davis
President/CEO, MVPwork LLC
Founder of Leading In High Heels Domestic Violence Non-profit
Best Selling Author: Boss Moves: How to think bigger, go harder and live better
Atlanta, GA

ACKNOWLEDGEMENTS

It has been a joyful journey in writing this book. I am grateful to God for granting me the gifts, talents, time, and passion to inspire and motivate others to live their lives with purpose. I wrote this book because the people who entrusted me to mentor, manage, and motivate them convinced me that many others could benefit from the *40 achievement principles* that I have imparted in them over the years. Affectionately known as "My Motivators," there are too many of these individuals to name, but there are a few that truly have been the wind beneath my wings for many years *(in alphabetical order):* Ainka, Aleisha, Anthony, Bridgette, Cheron, Christy, Crystal, Daniel, Donna, Elandis, Erika, Felicia, Gwen, Heidi, Jamiria, Jennifer, Larry, LaTesha, LaTorsha, Leslie, Michael, Michelle, Neena, Nicola, Reinette, Robert, Symeon, Syreeta, Tamarrah, Tekla, Terrance, and Tiffany.

I want to thank all of my sorority sisters with whom I've shared this important body of work for being a great source of inspiration. This book's cover design is dedicated to you.

I want to thank Becky A. Davis who convinced me to join her in the wonderful world of executive coaching. She is truly the big sister I always wanted growing up.

Self-publishing is a beast. But I was surrounded by the best. Thank you Elaine Young, William C. Jones, Eric "Bo" Foston, and Gwen Julien for your cover design work, copy, and content edits.

I thank my soul mate and spiritual partner for seeing me just as I am and motivating me to "finish strong." Kelly Robinson, you are my HERO!

I extend a special thank you to my soror and "momager," Mildred Skipwith Drayton. Thank you for supporting me personally and professionally, and for attending every major "Dr. Quinn Motivates" and "TEAM-MOE" event since I began this journey.

I want to thank my best friend, soror, confidant, and trusted advisor of 38 years and counting, Tyronda Minter, who loves, laughs, and lifts me up through it all. You are the epitome of true sisterhood and authentic friendship.

PREFACE

A cursory narrative of my life's story begins with being born to a teen mother and absent father; and ultimately raised by my maternal aunt and 4th grade-educated grandmother under very difficult socio-economic conditions. Living in a lower-income neighborhood also relegated me to attend statistically underperforming public schools.

Nevertheless, I pause to extend my gratitude to extended family, teachers, early childhood church youth leaders, mentors, and community dance and drama program coaches for giving me the best of the best of what they had to offer. I wholeheartedly contend that their collective influences gave me the courage to choose the road less traveled. Their teachings and guidance ultimately resulted in me being the recipient of academic scholarships to top-ranking universities, landing coveted positions in prestigious government and corporate organizations, and receiving professional honors and accolades.

Over the years I have had the privilege to network with powerful, prestigious women and executives, and rubbed shoulders with industry and community leaders, government officials and even celebrities. Yes, this little girl from the hood was living the life of a person who seemingly overcame insurmountable odds and obstacles – from poverty to peak achievements, or so I thought.

I remember vividly the day and perhaps even the exact hour my journey along the road less traveled veered into the proverbial "valley of the shadow of death." What I feared most during that dark period is all that I had accomplished and worked vehemently to overcome would now land me in the "mediocre middle." I longed for more but didn't quite know how to break away from the middle of the pack without being socially isolated and selling my soul to fiercely compete in the cut-throat culture of corporate America. Don't get me wrong, the middle of the road is both financially and socially comfortable; however I knew I had far more potential than to settle for the "ordinary average."

While existing in the valley someone suggested that I read Iyanla Vanzant's book, "One Day My Soul Just Opened Up." It was my first exposure to spiritual life counseling. Being a staunch student and lifelong learner, I committed to complete the 40 days and 40 nights of homework recommended by Vanzant. Through intense insightful reflection I came to the realization there is value in the valley and a purpose for every struggle. Coincidentally, Vanzant later published a book titled, "Value in the Valley."

At the conclusion of the 40 days of soul-searching I felt lighter and invigorated, and emerged with greater clarity concerning: (1) who I was (at that time); (2) what I was not, and perhaps most importantly; (3) who I could become through commitment and perseverance to rise beyond the valley of mediocrity. All the challenges and hardships that originally led to shame, resentment, guilt, anger, and fear of the future were converted to confidence, courage, faith, fortitude, optimism, and an unparalleled resolve to press forward to reach my full potential.

Throughout the years I have consciously incorporated Vanzant's spiritual principles into my own daily living. The process of reading, studying, practicing, and sharing outcomes with others eventually morphed into a workshop where I share *40 achievement principles* within the life-changing concepts of: (1) inspiration; (2) reconciliation; (3) confirmation; (4) transformation; and (5) motivation. The end result of studying Vanzant's works, reading hundreds of books, and studying the lives of high achieving people also gave birth to "Dr. Quinn Motivates" – my own brand of life coaching and motivation.

After penning this book I noted the acronyms used over the five chapters ironically add up to *40 achievement principles.* I view this as a significant connection since it reminds me of the 40 days and 40 nights I spent internalizing the 40 principles presented by Vanzant in "One Day My Soul Just Opened Up."

The motivational summaries and workbook activities that follow draw heavily from my studies on highly successful people. As a gift to you I transformed the works of others into tools, templates, and activities to make the *40 achievement principles* pertinent for you. It is my hope that you will do the work to change everything blocking you from living a life of amazing creativity and high achievement in direct proportion to your God-given talents and potential.

Let's Go!
Dr. Quinn Motivates

INTRODUCTION

The literary marketplace is saturated with self-help books on almost every aspect of life. Diverse topics include health and wellness, lifestyle management, leadership, entrepreneurship, financial and money management, spirituality, and let's not exclude the unprecedented market share owned by books on love and relationships. With such a plethora of available material and information on self-improvement, the question must be raised: Why do so many people still fall short of living their lives to the fullest potential and in harmony with their soul's desire?

In order to reach your fullest potential and live a life of excellence, a key assumption is that you will commit to doing the intensive, individualized work necessary to transform your life. After all, "you can't change what you refuse to confront." The *40 achievement principles* contained in this book sets it apart from others because of its inspirational appeal and customized action planning process designed specifically for you. Collectively, this approach furnishes guidance on how to pursue a purpose-driven life.

The *40 achievement principles* are aimed to challenge you to soul search and connect intimately with your passions. It is anticipated that you will confront seemingly impractical, uncomfortable, radical choices that will change your life as you reinvent yourself to live the life you desire. For some, it may mean finally completing the college degree put on hold. For others, it may mean making the decision to start a business. While for some, it may mean walking away from unhealthy relationships.

The *40 achievement principles* have also been attributed to guiding people away from a life scripted for them to living a life uniquely designed by them. Sadly, achievement in our society has become synonymous with the pride of climbing the corporate ladder, earning lots of money, and living a life of luxury. From my perspective, you can have all of the above, yet still feel inadequate. The *40 achievement principles* promote living a life you are passionate about, not necessarily one that will make you wealthy.

In my readings and examination of highly successful people, I discovered many do not consider themselves as "successful". In their minds they were either unhappy or felt they had missed the mark in living at full capacity.

Paradoxically, these individuals have many external markers and material possessions symbolizing success, yet they view themselves as underachieving largely because there is a lack of joy. In essence, they are not living a life of purpose and passion. What I concluded from their lives, as well as my own, is that achievement is about being happy from deep within. If achievement is defined as steps on a ladder, then chasing success will take on the life of an addict chasing the next high. I believe that if you live comfortably and work in a field or capacity that brings you joy and fulfillment, then you are living up to your full potential.

Among those applying the *40 achievement principles,* I have witnessed successful corporate executives quit six (6) figure careers to cater nutritious foods to daycare facilities and summer school programs, pursue their dreams in the arts, start mentoring programs in underprivileged communities, and one became a flight attendant to see the majestic wonders of the world. I have observed doctors leave lucrative private practices and corporate settings to provide healthcare in underserved communities in rural and inner-city America, and in third world countries. I have also witnessed successful Wall Street investors pursue full time careers in teaching, the arts, or ministry. These individuals made such radical choices only after understanding that achievement is attained by aligning your everyday life with your dreams. Just as with these individuals, I am interested in challenging you to commit to the process of transforming your life into the one you have always wanted. Yes, you may lose some people and choose to leave others along the way. But the pursuit of purpose is not a popularity contest - it is about living up to your God-given potential.

A few people have hired me as a life coach with the hidden motive of looking for the equivalent of a magic potion of motivation for springing into actions towards higher levels of creativity and achievement. I don't work magic or miracles, nor do I fix broken lives. You must do the work to fix your own life. You must answer questions posed throughout this book for yourself, and customize your own action plan for transformation. You have to unpack your own past and create an achievement program for your own future.

It is important to recognize and internalize that you have everything you need to achieve your God-given purpose. My hope is that you have the courage to separate yourself from the middle of the pack and embrace your full potential. Regardless of the current stage of your life, I have one word of advisement: Persevere! As you undertake the quest to achieve living your best life, resolve to push beyond challenges and obstacles with an attitude and expectation that you will win.

When we cling to people, places, and things that no longer serve a purpose in our life, we make change more difficult. Begin by detoxing on comfort and complacency in exchange for an elixir of vulnerability and transparency. Just like the butterfly, your life can be transformed to bring forth your most brilliant self. In keeping with the butterfly analogy, you must go through distinct phases of struggle, strength, and freedom in preparation to soar towards greatness. If you incorporate these concepts into your everyday life, what once seemed insurmountable becomes vividly achievable.

We are all created with an enormous capacity for creativity and achievement. However, in order to actualize it we must embark upon a purpose-driven journey. The pursuit of purpose is never achieved on the straight and narrow. Instead, you must be willing to take the "road less traveled" which is unpaved, and invariably characterized by twists, turns, bumps, and bends. To succeed along the road less traveled requires an "I can't return to mediocrity" mentality. I sincerely believe this book will energize and inspire you to courageously address barriers blocking your road to success.

Although you and I may never meet, our spirits have already crossed paths. The fact that you are reading this book suggests we are kindred spirits yearning to grow and create a life of significance. I am honored and privileged to serve as your motivator and will be equally inspired by your courage to take action in planning and achieving your goals. There is no better time than the present to commit to fulfilling your utmost potential. Don't procrastinate. Do what you have to do to rekindle your lost dreams and revitalize your enthusiasm for life.

Let's Go to Work!

Dr. Quinn Motivates

INSPIRATION

"The process of being mentally stimulated to do or feel something"

"Without inspiration you lack motivation. Without motivation you lack determination. Without determination you settle into a comfort zone and cope by "justifying" and then "just lying" about why you are not living up to your full potential."

Dr. Quinn Motivates

Your gifts, talents, callings, personality, and life experiences are unique. Your uniqueness makes it difficult to precisely know the exact formula for optimizing your potential. This is why it is imperative that you access diverse sources of inspiration for motivation to maximize your creativity and potential for higher achievement. Inspiration unleashes your inner vision, wisdom, and strength to create the life you have always imagined. When coupled with transparency and vulnerability, inspiration sparks a childlike optimism that empowers you to alleviate any self-limiting talk and doubt.

The right blend of diverse sources of inspiration can revitalize your belief that your dreams can come true. However, in order to benefit fully from diverse forms of inspiration, it is imperative that you commit to do the work to be engaged fully in the process of discovering what it takes to achieve your full potential. This degree of authentic inspiration requires that you invest ample time and attention to be connected deeply to that which your soul desires. The work that follows inspiration can be uncomfortable at times because our formal educational system has conditioned us to sit down and be "taught" or rather "told" what to think with very little emphasis on application. It is your responsibility, therefore, to figure out a game plan for maximizing your potential once inspired to do something different with your life.

WHERE DOES "INSPIRATION" COME FROM?

I am often asked, "How do you know when you have encountered true inspiration?" In my work I have discovered that inspiration flows primarily from three broad sources: (1) divine inspiration from God; (2) inspiration that flows to you from others; and (3) inspiration imbedded in your own life experiences of overcoming odds and obstacles.

Divine inspiration. Inspiration in its most sacred form is God's voice. To derive inspiration from God's voice entails reading God's inspired word for yourself and listening to others as they properly interpret and apply God's word. Divine inspiration is magnified when hearing and reading the word of God balanced with prayer. Prayer is summarized as sharing your feelings with God, thanking God for blessing you and providing for you, asking God for forgiveness and continued supplication, and asking God to reveal your life's purpose. Once you have shared with God your sincere desires and dreams, you have to be available to receive and accept God's response, as "divine timing."

Being inspired by others. From an earthly perspective, there is nothing more inspiring than to become intimately acquainted with the back stories of those we celebrate as captains of industry, creative geniuses, and top performers in their respective fields of sports, entertainment, business, and even community advocacy. I am especially intrigued in learning the details of how successful people overcame odds and obstacles that would have been more than enough to justify ending their pursuit of higher aspirations. I want to caution you that to be inspired by someone else's story is one thing; however to be moved to apply their methods, procedures, and discipline takes on another level of commitment that transcends initial inspiration. I am constantly reminding people that you may want my outcomes, but are you willing to commit to my process. The essence of being inspired by others' stories of strength, struggle, survival, and success is to commit fully to the work to put inspiration into action.

Inspired by your own life experiences. As human beings seeking to protect ourselves, we often bury life's episodes and experiences that were disappointing, embarrassing, humiliating, painful, and shameful. During those times we are desperately preoccupied with putting painful memories at a cognitive and physical distance so we can show up as "normal" as possible in the world within which we live, work, play, and perhaps worship. What we fail to recognize, however, is that we actually are rejecting the seeds of strength and resilience that manifest as our own brand of "homegrown inspiration." In fact, several noted psychologists have suggested that many artists in particular find sources of inspiration to create what we eventually refer to as "masterpieces," "innovation," "technological breakthroughs," "game changers," or "revolutionary", were birthed simply from revisiting unresolved psychological conflict or childhood trauma. In like manner, I believe that when you give yourself permission to explore experiences that at the time brought you seemingly unbearable hurt, pain, and shame, you will unpack buried treasures that are extremely valuable as you prepare to pursue higher goals.

I have presented to you three (3) primary sources of inspiration. No matter the source, there are some proven methods for being fully present to maximize diverse types of inspirational encounters.

1. *Sit still.* Inspiration requires you to resist the need to "do" and embrace the need to "be still" and know that something divine is happening from the inside out. The art is to learn the discipline of sitting for longer periods of time without labeling it as daydreaming or a waste of time.

2. *Silence your thoughts.* Inspiration flows best when you are able to silence random and racing thoughts long enough to take in the full range of what you are experiencing as you encounter environments, people, and things that inspire you. Silencing your thoughts is a way of whispering to your soul's desire that it is safe to come forward.

3. *Observe.* Learning to observe for inspirational purposes is more difficult than you may think because we have been programmed to analyze, judge, and give meaning to situations as a way to show we are "knowledgeable." Inspiration that comes from simply observing your

surroundings teaches you to have a greater appreciation at face value for your life experiences. In addition, you learn to have more compassion for people as you observe them in their natural element living and coping as best they can with whatever resources they have.

4. *Listen.* Of all the ways to be inspired, listening is the one we think we have under control. However, our tendency is to confuse listening with hearing. Hearing is simply the act of perceiving sound by the ear. If you are not hearing-impaired, hearing simply happens. Listening, however, is something you consciously choose to do. Listening requires concentration so that your brain processes meaning from words and sentences. Furthermore, even among those who master listening, there is still the need to comprehend. Listening for inspiration is a combination of accepting a conversation at face value and without interruption. Listening is optimized when it is matched with keen observation.

5. *Read.* In my opinion, social media has become the enemy of reading for comprehension. Social media's memes of sound bites have replaced deeper study and research. Even though I have succumbed to using memes to remain relevant in today's social media market, it is not my favorite option. As a traditionalist, I still believe sitting down with a good book on a topic of interest is a far greater form of inspiration than poppy cock inspiration in the form of memes. I also recommend reading the classics in your area of interest and expertise.

6. *Write.* Another great tool for inspiration is to journal your original thoughts. Journaling without fear can result in some of the most profound opportunities for self-healing, detoxing on old paradigms, and paving the way for creating new thoughts. Most people filter their writings primarily for fear of someone else reading their attempts to be free, honest, vulnerable, and transparent. To help you get started in this regard, at the end of each achievement principle are blank lines to write your feelings, thoughts, and action plans for application.

7. *Explore.* Sometimes we get stuck looking to the same people, places, and things to inspire us. It is important to give yourself permission to wander aimlessly into parts of the world that would normally be off your radar screen. Visit new places. Attend diverse events. Meet people you wouldn't normally speak to during your daily routine.

8. *Communicate.* Find trusted individuals with whom you can share your feelings, thoughts, and creative hunches. Some examples include Mastermind groups, and professional mentoring groups. Mastermind

groups offer a combination of masterminding, peer brainstorming, education, accountability and support in a group setting among equally ambitious individuals. The beauty of Mastermind Groups is that participants raise the bar by challenging each other to create and implement goals, brainstorm ideas, and support each other with total honesty, respect, and compassion. Plan to meet regularly with an agenda sometimes, and at other times just to talk out your ideas and brainstorm. At the inspiration phase, steer clear of interacting with people who are critical, have tunnel-vision, or are overly analytical. Structured thinkers have their place and role to shape and execute, but they can be a disruption during the inspiration phase.

9. *Create.* Begin the process of creating new thoughts and new things as they are revealed to you through various forms of inspiration. Create vision boards, doodle, sketch, or even tape record to allow the flow of creativity to be uninterrupted by reality or structure. Once your thoughts are all out of your brain in some shape or form, you will need to take on a more project management approach to move innovative ideas along the continuum of development. Joining a vision board group is a great way to jumpstart the creative process, especially if you never thought of yourself as creative in the way it is commonly defined in our society as synonymous with being artistic.

The greatest inspiration comes from personalizing the *40 achievement principles* in this book. You must begin the process with a deep desire for continuous learning and be courageous enough to act on the new knowledge. To do so, you need a vigorous determination to explore and eliminate everything that is no longer serving your greater purpose.

WHEN INSPIRATION GIVES WAY TO AN EPIPHANY, GO WITH IT!

The best case scenario of inspiration is to experience an epiphany, which is described as a moment when you suddenly realize that you understand, or suddenly become conscious of, something that is very important to you. Also known as an "aha moment," an epiphany sparked by inspiration is a game changer when it comes to setting the stage for reaching one's potential. Although they are thought to appear suddenly, the reality is epiphanies often are the result of significant work on the part of the discoverer. In this chapter, I elaborate upon seven (7) of the *40 achievement principles* associated closely with being inspired. However, if you get an epiphany as you immerse yourself in the work of being inspired, go with it!

PRINCIPLES FOR INSPIRATION	
I	INSIGHT
N	NURTURE
S	SELF-AWARENESS
P	PASSION
I	INTUITION
R	RELATIONSHIPS
E	EXPLORATION

Let's Go to Work!

INSPIRATION: SUGGESTED PLAYLIST

Song *(Artist)*

1. Chariots of Fire *(Vangelis)*
2. Beautiful *(Christina Aguilera)*
3. What a Wonderful World *(Louis Armstrong)*
4. Don't Stop Believin' *(Journey)*
5. Imagine *(John Lennon)*
6. Hello Fear *(Kirk Franklin)*
7. Somewhere Over the Rainbow *(Kimberly Locke)*
8. Expression *(Salt n Pepa)*
9. Have You Seen My Childhood *(Michael Jackson)*
10. The Greatest Love of All *(Whitney Houston)*
11. Tomorrow *(Annie Soundtrack)*
12. Let It Go *(Frozen Soundtrack)*
13. Against All Odds *(Phil Collins)*
14. Arthur's Theme: Best That You Can Do *(Christopher Cross)*
15. Pure Imagination *(Willy Wonka)*
16. Smile *(Michael Jackson)*
17. The Voice Within *(Christina Aguilera)*
18. One Moment in Time *(Whitney Houston)*
19. You're the Inspiration *(Chicago)*
20. Man in the Mirror *(Michael Jackson)*

INSIGHT

"Insight in its purest form demands that you be fully present and in the moment that truth is being revealed to you."

Dr. Quinn Motivates

Insight is internalizing that which inspires you. As you embark upon new and innovative ways to be inspired, sit still long enough to gain some insight from that which you are listening to and observing. Resist the desire to respond or react initially. Instead, commit to the discipline of "taking it all in" and sorting through what makes sense for your life's journey. Insight is optimized when your body and mind are rested and you are open to dig deep into your soul in search of a connection to that which you really desire.

Insight is personal and potentially painful. Many avoid seeking authentic insight because they are afraid of addressing what they may discover as the causes and consequences of not living up to one's full potential. Gaining insight later in life can spark resentment and regret when you come face to face with the people and circumstances that were part of the reason why you have yet to achieve your greatest potential. However, the greatest benefit of insight is that of discovering the full truth of who you are and what you are capable of achieving. The clarity brought on by insight helps you release any barriers and limitations that have held you back. In addition, a deeper dive into insight will help you to become aware of your own decisions that alienated you from that which you are passionate about.

Insight broadens your vision. The end goal of a sincere effort to gain insight should be vision. The problem is people try to stop prematurely the rigorous process of applying inspiration in ways that ignites insight. Instead, they tend to want to get moving expeditiously on action plans and results. I suggest that you give yourself permission to dwell in your safe space of "insight" where ideas and the ideal flow through you uncompromised, unapologetically, and untainted by others. Instead, allow insight to help you internalize for yourself that which you could be if only you start believing in the seemingly impossible or insurmountable.

It's Time to Go to Work: "Insight"

"The dreamers are the saviors of the world."
James Allen

British philosophical writer James Allen penned "As a Man Thinketh" in the midst of the very explosive and exploitative Industrial Revolution. Although first articulated in 1903, Allen's framework is still quite relevant in gaining "insight" on what really matters most in your life. His spirit was grieved as he witnessed capitalism dominate the political economy. His work quietly gained momentum as a way to maintain internal sanity and stay grounded mentally. His principles on maintaining character and integrity are particularly useful if you work in a cut-throat corporate culture where authentic creativity and innovation take a back seat to increasing shareholder wealth by any means necessary.

1. **CHARACTER:** What are your core values and life philosophy to avoid compromising them?

2. **THE IMPACT OF CIRCUMSTANCES ON ONE'S LIFE CHOICES:** How have certain circumstances (political, economic, religious, education, and family) resulted in choices that compromised your core values?

3. **HEALTH AND THE BODY:** What is your regimen for cleansing and detoxing your mind and body?

4. **PURPOSE:** What is your central purpose? What methodology are you using to document the details of your purpose-driven life as it is revealed to you?

5. **ACHIEVEMENT FACTORS:** What is your process for being personally responsible for maintaining high moral standards as you pursue higher aspirations?

6. **VISION AND DREAMS:** What are your visions and dreams? Are you willing to take on the persona of a "composer," "sculptor," "painter," "poet," or "prophet" where the emphasis is on creating and crafting new thoughts and things?

7. **SERENITY:** When in environments that are filled with conflict, chaos, and confusion, how do you calm your spirit and mind as a way to remain connected to your core values?

Nurture

"Nurture is about who 'cared' for you and is not to be confused with who 'raised' you."
Dr. Quinn Motivates

Parental nurturing styles at a glance. Nurturing is about who cared for you emotionally and socially, while raising a child is about who provided for you and regulated your behavior. Taking a transparent look at the ways in which you were nurtured and raised can unlock some reasons why you have stopped short of being "all in" towards pursuing your dream. If you were reared by a primarily "dominant parent," then you experienced all management in your household where there was very little tolerance for rule breaking and perhaps extreme punishment for minor offenses. Those who grew up with "influential parents" may have experienced the softer side of a dominant parent. By this I mean, the influential parent still wants to raise a high-achieving child, but they often are not as hard, although probably every bit as demanding in other ways on the child as the dominant parent. Children raised by "servant parents" get the most nurturing of all as these parents are sensitive, patient, and great listeners, but they can be smothering and overprotective. The final major nurturing style is "conscientious parents", who typically are teachers, preachers, and politicians. The children of these parents tend to be morally responsible and reflect "good family" values, but may be forced to live a double life of hiding family secrets and dysfunctions.

Negative nurturing experiences have their purpose. In studying the lives of high-achieving individuals, I discovered that many grew up in households that were less than ideal. Recurring parental struggles most endured included: (1) absenteeism; (2) addiction; (3) unfaithfulness; (4) violence; (5) chronic illness; (6) limited education and employment; (7) chronic homelessness; (8) overbearing/smothering; (9) neglectful; and (10) trying to be best friends with their children. In the end, never underestimate the strengths and resilience gained from having learned to survive in a household that was less than ideal.

It's Time to Go to Work: "Nurture"

"Pampering is about making a shift to integrating experiences and making choices in your life that bring you joy, peace, and pleasure."

Debrena Jackson-Gandy

So many people re-traumatize themselves in a desperate attempt to demand that those who were supposed to provide nurturing and guidance admit they failed, and commit to make up for the lack of nurturing during the formative years. For a number of reasons, live your life in such a way that you never expect to get closure as to why the adults assigned to care for you did not fulfill their obligations. Instead, resolve to commit to nurturing yourself later in life. Bestselling author about self-care, Debrena Jackson-Gandy, provides the best advice in nurturing the hurting inner child as you transition to fulfill greater aspiration.

JACKSON-GANDY'S SUGGESTIONS FOR NURTURING YOURSELF LATER IN LIFE

1. Address and reject the need to live up to the myth and reality of the "strong black woman syndrome" or any other myths that might have been inherited
2. Reflect upon what brings you joy now and compare that list with what brought you joy as a child under age 13
3. Fall in love with yourself by dating yourself
4. Tune up your spirit through prayer and meditation
5. Make peace with your body
6. Create sacred spaces and places to practice self-care and success rituals
7. Free yourself from "dis-ease" before it evolves into "disease"

The promise of self-pampering: According to Jackson-Gandy, pampering results in a shift in mindset and deep-seated beliefs in key areas of wholeness:

1. Self-image
2. Love relationships
3. Body
4. Appearance
5. Friendships
6. Marriage
7. Interactions with [your] children
8. Energy level
9. Productivity
10. Sex life

Self-Awareness

"Only a fully integrated self is prepared to honestly answer the question: "Who am I?"
Dr. Quinn Motivates

Inspiration from others opens you to self-awareness. Creative thinkers and high achievers maximize their potential by becoming fully self-aware. Self-awareness is going deep into who you are as opposed to believing who people told you that you are. Becoming fully self-aware requires what I call "executive sessions with self" where you do the hard work comprised of "head work" and "heart work" to sort through the basic question of "Who am I?" These "executive sessions with self" allow you to fully own the truth about yourself, how you see the world, and what you believe is possible for your future.

Self-awareness is a blend of vulnerability and courage. A comprehensive perspective on self-awareness prepares your soul to be open to see yourself as you really are and have the courage to change those things that do not fully represent who you are and what you desire to become. If you desire to keep secrets, are in denial, or have succumbed to a selected memory that leaves your victim status intact, you are not ready for a comprehensive process of self-awareness. Only an open soul is ready for a rigorous, raw, vulnerable, and fully transparent examination of all that you are from the inside-out.

Self-awareness includes accepting the good, the bad, and the untapped potential of who you are. Becoming aware of yourself and your potential for significance is a courageous pursuit because it includes facing those unpleasant aspects of yourself that you hide to avoid criticism and exposure. However, persistent cover up of less flattering dimensions of you over time result in a shut-down of important parts of yourself that thwart your creativity and achievement. You have to be willing to examine every experience, incident, and entanglement in an effort to answer honestly the "Who am I?" question. As a starting point I invite you to use my "40 Dimensions of Self" that follow on the next page.

IT'S TIME TO GO TO WORK: "SELF-AWARENESS"

"What lies behind us and what lies before us are tiny matters compared to what lies within us."

Oliver Wendell Holmes

The self-awakening exercise: Use "Dr. Quinn's comprehensive self-awareness framework" to transform through key phases of increased self-awareness as follows: (1) avoidance; (2) awareness; (3) acceptance; (4) awakening; (5) action; (6) actualization; and (7) achievement.

DR. QUINN'S 40 DIMENSIONS OF A COMPREHENSIVE SELF-AWARENESS FRAMEWORK			
GOOD SELF	SOCIAL CONSTRUCTION OF SELF	BAD SELF	OPEN TO CHANGING ONESELF
1. Self- worth	11. Self-consciousness	21. Self- pity	31. Self-reflection
2. Self-efficacy	12. Sexual/intimate self	22. Self-centered	32. Self-assessment
3. Self-valuation	13. Social self	23. Self-sabotage	33. Self-discovery
4. Self-preservation	14. Self-talk	24. Self-denial	34. Self-acceptance
5. Self-affirmation	15. Self-disposition	25. Self-imposed limitations	35. Self-scripting
6. Self-respect	16. Self-identity	26. Self-serving	36. Self- awakening
7. Self-love	17. Self-esteem	27. Self-doubt	37. Self-disclosure
8. Self-healing	18. Self-presentation	28. Self-rejection	38. Self-actualization
9. Self-will	19. Self-image	29. Self-avoidance	39. Self-determination
10. Self-empowerment	20. The looking glass self	30. Self-hatred	40. Self-fulfillment

The opened soul exercise. For continued work in self-awareness, I recommend exploring Iyanla Vanzant's 40 concepts of an "opened soul". Her work is particularly helpful if you are open to addressing barriers that limit you from higher levels of achievement.

Notes to Self on "Self-awareness"

PURPOSE & PASSION

"Find your passion and it will reveal your purpose."
Dr. Quinn Motivates

There is a direct correlation between purpose and passion. Inspiration brings clarity to your life's purpose, and serves as fuel for moving you closer to that which brings you optimal joy. Thinking about what you do well is a starting point for clarifying purpose and bringing you closer to that which you are passionate about. Passion is not about working extreme hours and neglecting your personal responsibilities and social life. In fact, those who are passionate about their work have more time, energy, and resources to enjoy the things that add value to their total quality of life. There are four (4) components to draw inspiration as you seek clarity in your life's purpose.

1. *Gifts and talents:* Identify what you are naturally good at and can do with little effort.

2. *Trained knowledge:* Document all the formal training you have undertaken to sharpen your gifts and talents.

3. *Skills:* Identify activities you do well with repetition, but may not be formally trained in.

4. *Passion:* Pinpoint things that you genuinely enjoy doing because it brings personal fulfillment.

There is no such thing as being too late in life to live out your purpose. If you think you have missed your opportunity to pursue your purpose, I challenge you to muster up the courage to begin again. Unfortunately, by the time many people discover what their purpose entails, they have spent a greater portion of their lives making more practical decisions that could leave your purpose seemingly out of reach. If you are one of those people who have missed key opportunities to pursue your purpose, you could benefit from working with a life coach familiar with your field and interest to get you back on track. Be sure you take into account innovative ways to manage multiple priorities and responsibilities as you pursue your purpose later in life.

It's Time to Go to Work: "Purpose & Passion"

"You could reach all your personal goals, become a raving success by the world's standard, and still miss the purposes for which God created you."
Rick Warren

The following are three (3) activities to help you connect purpose and passion.

RICK WARREN'S PURPOSE-DRIVEN LIFE. If you are in search of your "calling" also known as "one's purpose for life", I recommend you begin with reading The Purpose-Driven Life by Rick Warren, an American evangelical Christian pastor and author. This spiritually-guided journey is a 40-day process aimed at answering the most important question of one's life: "What on Earth are you Here For?"

NAPOLEON HILL'S PROCESS FOR DISCOVERING AND ACHIEVING ONE'S PURPOSE. Mr. Hill, one of America's foremost success/motivation authors, stated in "Think and Grow Rich" that the principal reasons some people succeed and others fail is that successful people have a definite purpose for their lives. He outlined the following four (4) steps for helping individuals identify a definitive purpose.

1. Write down a clear, concise statement of what you want most.
2. Develop an outline of your plan to achieve this major goal. Then turn those written goals into something visual, such as a "vision board."
3. Set timetables for achieving goals tied to your overall purpose.
4. Memorize your chief goals and plans and affirm them daily through "self-talk."

BECKY DAVIS'S PERSPECTIVE ON CONNECTING PASSION AND PURPOSE. Ms. Davis is a highly respected and sought after business coach who outlines strategies for putting your purpose into action using a methodology she branded as the "p-factors" as follows:

1. The Process: Plug in, Promises, Purpose, and Practice
2. The Picture: Paint it
3. The Project: People, Play, Pondering skills, Pow-wows
4. Participation: Partnership, Provision
5. Progression: Persuasion, Professional development, Personal development, the Pay off

NOTES TO SELF ON "PURPOSE & PASSION"

INTUITION

"Intuition is an inspirational message from the soul."

Dr. Quinn Motivates

Intuition is being inspired by that which is already inside you. You must learn to trust your gut which means applying the knowledge that you have acquired through life's experiences. Ralph Waldo Emerson once said "Tomorrow a stranger will say with masterly good sense precisely what we have thought and felt all the time." Emerson's insight pinpoints the exact reason why so many brilliant, God-gifted individuals fall short of reaching their full potential. We have been programmed to fear our intuition as a form of defence mechanism, source of stability, and protection rather than as a force to propel us to greater heights. Not only must you learn to trust your gut, but you must get the courage to speak and act on what comes to you as intuition.

Intuition is communicating with yourself on a deeper level, assessing the possibilities of your choices, and thinking through the likely consequences. Intuition is knowing when to disengage to avoid unpleasant experiences. Intuition serves as a wise and compassionate guide that is always available to you. Intuition is getting out of your head and in touch with your gut. You can only utilize the gift of intuition fully if you are willing to become fully aware of what you are feeling.

When applied properly, intuition helps you distinguish between an opportunity and danger, truth and lies, and right and wrong. The key is to courageously act quickly on intuition. Ignoring your intuition and resolving to wait on more information can result in your missing major opportunities towards maximizing your potential for achievement. Intuition is diminished when you want to rely heavily on knowledge or you have an emotional blockage that leads to inability to tap into intuition. Honor the emotional cleansing process as a way to detox feelings that impair self-esteem, relationships, and daily activities. When you block emotions, negativity oozes out or disease sets inside the body.

It's time to go to Work: "Intuition"

"Your time is limited, so don't waste it living someone else's life. Don't be trapped by dogma - which is living with the results of other people's thinking. Don't let the noise of others' opinions drown out your own inner voice. And most important, have the courage to follow your heart and intuition."

Steve Jobs

Many live limited lives because they do not trust their gut about what actions to take. Review the list below and identify times when you should have relied upon your intuition to guide your decision-making progress.

1. Intimate partner selection
2. Educational and enrichment endeavors
3. Career and business ventures
4. Financial planning and big ticket item purchases
5. Health and wellness choices

In reading Gary Zukav's work on "intuition," I identified the following action steps for increasing one's reliance upon the power of intuition in making important life-changing decisions.

1. Be still long enough to become aware of what you are feeling in a particular moment.
2. Recognize historical knowledge imbedded in past experiences and take full responsibility for acting upon what you already know to be true.
3. Commit to emotional cleansing to eliminate "emotional blockages" as a way to increase your willingness to trust what you are feeling.
4. Embark upon a physical and nutritional cleansing regimen that frees your body of toxins that interfere with intuition.
5. Honor and trust wise counsel that comes to confirm that which you already know.
6. Trust that all that is happening in and around you is working for your good even if it doesn't look or feel good in the natural flow of life.
7. Trust your intuition as a reliable source for revealing "truth" and then have the guts to act on the truth.

RELATIONSHIPS

"Real relationships are sacred and require the sacrifice of heart work and head work which is hard work... but it would be so easy if we simply knew on the front end which was real and worth the sacrifice."

Dr. Quinn Motivates

Relationships can ignite or dull inspiration. As creative thinkers committed to achieving your highest potential, you must understand that who you invite into your intimate space can make or break your spirit to excel. Resist the need to "do" anything or "say" anything to your significant others as you process past and present intimate relationships. This is simply your time to gain clarity in your own heart and mind. Later in the reconciliation phase, you will have the opportunity to explore actions that need to be taken in intimate relationships. It is at that time you should begin to think about your gentle, but firm approach to transforming relationships that are no longer bringing you joy.

Reflect on past relationship choices. As you reflect on your past relationships, think deeply about how unresolved issues of loss, abandonment, rejection, co-dependency, cheating, or lack of closure might be hindering your willingness to make healthy choices in relationships.

Evaluate intimate partners prior to serious commitment. Before comedian, radio and television personality "Uncle" Steve Harvey advised us on how to think about love, relationships, intimacy, and commitment, Dr. Gwendolyn Goldsby Grant, a noted media psychologist, gave us the following checklist for evaluating potential intimate partners: (1) Does he treat his mother with respect?; (2) Does he respect other women in his life?; (3) Does he have a Godly-consciousness?; (4) Does he have a work ethic?; (5) Does he have strong ties to his family and his community?; (6) Is he honest and kind?; (7) Does he have self-respect and good manners?; (8) Does he have high ideals and plans for the future?; (9) Does he understand the importance of communication?; (10) Is he in good health, and is he honest about his health?; (11) Is he able to compromise?; (12) Is he supportive and cooperative?; and (13) Does he act like you are a priority in his life?

It's time to go to Work: "Relationships"

"Without commitment you cannot learn to care for another person more than yourself. You cannot learn to value the growth of strength and clarity in another soul, even if that threatens the wants of your personality."

Gary Zukav

In reviewing Gary Zukav's work on relationships, I noted ten (10) dimensions of authentic relationships. Use these points to reflect upon past, present and future relationships in all areas of your life.

GARY ZUKAV'S KEY DIMENSIONS OF AUTHENTIC RELATIONSHIPS	
1. THE LAWS OF ATTRACTION	• You attract what you value. List your core values and weigh them against those of people you have intimate, social, and business relationships with to determine the extent to which there is harmony and conflict.
2. CONCEPTUALIZATION OF LOVE	• Recall how you developed a concept of love in your formative years. What you observed, heard, and were told love is became your socially-accepted definition of love.
3. CONCEPTUALIZATION OF COMMITMENT	• Just as with "love," you have a socially-constructed definition of "commitment."
4. GROWTH AND DEVELOPMENT	• Ideally, every relationship should contribute positively to your growth and development. Identify what you learned from ALL of your past significant relationships.
5. A SPIRIT OF COOPERATION WITH AND APPRECIATION	• Once you have done the work in points 1 – 4, you are now ready for selecting and entering future relationships that are built upon cooperation and appreciation as opposed to fear and doubt.
6. AUTHENTIC POWER	• Authentic power is a freedom from the inside out that allows two equally strong people to co-exist without dominating and exploiting one another.
7. INTERDEPENDENCY	• Interdependence is only a choice that independent people can make as each chooses to rely upon each other.
8. SPIRIT OF EQUALITY	• A spirit of equality begins with shared values, goals, and mutuality of purpose, also referred to as being "equally yoked" as two spirits move in the same direction, at a similar pace, and with a shared rhythm.
9. SHARED SEARCH FOR HEALING AND TRUST	• Authentic relationships provide a safe place for otherwise strong individuals to share concerns and insecurities in ways that contribute to each other's healing and enhanced trust.
10. MULTI-DIMENSIONAL COMPATIBILITY	• Multi-dimensional compatibility is best described as "chemistry" where people in committed relationships have shared values and goals, and enjoy each other in a number of areas, including spiritual, sexual, emotional, financial, professional, and recreational.

NOTES TO SELF ON "RELATIONSHIPS"

EXPLORATION

"It takes courage to explore the unfulfilled areas of your life."
Dr. Quinn Motivates

Inspiration often leads to a deeper desire to explore unfulfilled areas of your life. Commitment to exploration is the first step towards unleashing pent up creativity and potential for higher achievement. As you embark upon exploration, you begin to gain clarity to questions such as: (1) where do I really want to go from here in life?; and (2) what risks am I willing to take to get me there?

Exploration can occur through reading. My world of exploration was greatly broadened mentally, physically, socially and spiritually after reading Dr. Scott Peck's book "The Road Less Traveled." The first thing the book did for me was clarify that a life of discipline could co-exist with a life of exploration. After reading his book, I realized that the reason I was not easily fitting into certain sub-segments of society is because I was rejecting the scripts assigned to me based my interactions in various groups and settings. Using Dr. Peck's work, I began the process of re-scripting my life to align with my deepest desires. This resulted in me defining on my own terms: (1) how I would process problems and pains as phenomena that strengthened me, not parlayed me into a perpetual victim mentality; and (2) how I can delay instant gratification and take full responsibility for correcting shortcomings that stemmed from being a product of my environment. Dr. Peck's book also allowed me to open myself to new challenges, redefine love on multiple levels, commit to spiritual growth, and resolve in my soul that organized religion would forever be part of my life. I came to accept that I believe in grace, mercy and miracles. This level of enlightenment occurred over a long period of time and included many diverse types of exploration. However, the results were that I very well understood that life as I had come to know it was small. The world was my playground and I was curious enough to risk re-scripting my narrow role in society to play on a bigger world stage where I would have to use all my creative energy to maximize my potential.

It's Time to Go to Work: "Exploration"

"Someday when we have all had enough of spiritual growth in this human classroom, we will come to see that the various threads that have gone to make up this human life, the seemingly disjointed happenings, the jumble of events, the apparent accidents, were really a part of an orderly, beautiful and perfect pattern."

Robert Anthony

Exploration is giving yourself permission to discover a world that is greater than the one imposed upon you. As a way to inspire yourself to live your best life now, commit to exploring areas of your life and the world that you have taken for granted. Inspiration through exploration typically results in a desire to "re-script" your life's narrative on your terms. Here are my eight (8) steps to help jumpstart the re-scripting process.

DR. QUINN'S 8-STEPS FOR "RE-SCRIPTING" YOUR LIFE		
R	**REVISIT YOUR CHILDHOOD REALITY**	• Every good script writer does research. Put a date certain on the calendar where you will go back to your old neighborhood and gain a different perspective on how this environment impacted your younger vulnerable self.
E	**EMBRACE YOUR DESIRE FOR ENLIGHTENMENT**	• In childlike mode focus on the enjoyment of exploration and learn new things with the intention of being "enriched" and not "rich".
S	**SELECT SCENES AND SCENARIOS**	• List scenes and scenarios from your past life that brought you extreme pain as well as extreme joy.
C	**CAST THE CHARACTERS**	• List the people in your past life and the roles they played that are the most memorable no matter if the memories are good or bad.
R	**RECAST THE CHARACTERS**	• List the roles you want to play in life or ways you want to play current roles differently. • Cast the other characters that will play significant and minor roles in your "re-scripted" life.
I	**IDENTIFY THE IDEAL**	• Write the ideal ending scene for a movie based on your life story.
P	**PRACTICE YOUR NEW SCRIPT**	• Once you know how you want your story to end, then practice your lines every day.
T	**TELL A DIFFERENT STORY**	• Lights, Camera, Action! Identify a date when your re-scripted life will be unveiled in public. Remember, no matter what, the show must go on!

RECONCILIATION

"intentional efforts towards restoring relationships to the extent possible."

"Reconciliation begins with being committed to telling the truth, soul searching, and risking care-frontations."

Dr. Quinn Motivates

Creative thinkers and high achievers maximize their potential when they commit to the process of reconciliation. The bottom line is you need people in your life to function personally and professionally. The problem is in knowing who the right people are, as well as knowing when even the right people have reached their limits and liabilities as you continue to grow and press towards higher aspirations. For the most part, most of us have the capacity to identify and eliminate the wrong people without hesitation. The complexity of reconciliation centers on what to do with people who were "right" at significant times in your life, but are no longer purposeful, and perhaps are even causing major conflicts.

The reconciliation process works best when you are brave enough to un-silence your own suffering, as well as apologize for suffering you caused others. Honor the time needed to prepare for reconciliation and to see the process through. Examine your motives and agenda for seeking reconciliation. In fact, before you actually engage other people in the reconciliation process, commit to a time of reflecting deeply on all that you experienced with a person. Empty out shame, guilt, sadness, and anger associated with dysfunctional relationships in particular. Once you detox on negative emotions, you are able to focus on what really matters in terms of values and beliefs. Clarity of values and beliefs pave the way for embracing the *40 achievement principles* discussed throughout this book.

Remember that family and friends didn't sign up for this process towards radical and authentic transformation. Be okay with them not remembering the facts and events and experiences the same way you recall them. Just in case there are others that are significant that may reject the invitation to reconcile, it is imperative that you follow this exact order of reconciliation: (1) reconciliation with oneself; (2) with the Divine; and (3) and then with others.

RECONCILIATION WITH SELF

The reconciliation process begins as a solo activity where you intentionally explore and examine with a full commitment to truth-telling all that you have experienced with others who are significant. "To thine own self be true" is one of the most widely quoted lines from Shakespeare's play Hamlet in which a father is warning his son to not do anything that is detrimental to his own best interest. In like manner, the reconciliation process begins with self-care where you look inward and really get to know who you are and reconcile various pieces of your own broken life prior to engaging others. Without going deeper into who you are at the very core, there is no need to pursue reconciliation with others. Self-reconciliation is a complex and vulnerable work where you must commit to searching your own soul and asking yourself the very tough question of why is it that you do not consistently behave like you believe? And what is the work that needs to be done to achieve total harmony between your behaviors and actions and your belief system?

RECONCILIATION WITH THE DIVINE

Reconnect and clarify your relationship with your Higher Power within the context of how you experience spirituality. If your quest for success has caused your moral compass to shift, you must do the work to get back to a place of repentance and resetting. Make amends. Get clarity on your values and beliefs and use them as guiding principles in your actions.

RECONCILIATION WITH OTHERS OF SIGNIFICANCE

Reconciling with others centers on the need to clear the air of old relational issues to make room for new relationships on the other side of transformation. There are just some people and some issues that cannot be part of the journey forward. You have carried these burdens and been held an emotional hostage for as long as you can stand it.

Reconciliation with those who are significant in your life. The risk of the reconciliation process with others who are significant is that it could lead to a breakthrough or a breakdown. The cause of the broken relationship is major and if both people don't see the cause to be the same, it will be difficult to reconcile.

Reconciliation with someone who has a past or current addiction problem is difficult. Addiction in any shape, form, or fashion creates moral wreckage where people cheat, deny, lie, or steal in order to get and use their drug of choice. Often what's left behind is a trail of shattered relationships. This level of reconciliation may require objective third-party counseling or mediation.

The best case scenario is when you are engaged in reconciliation with a person who is cooperating with the process. This person typically has a genuine interest in a positive outcome to restore a broken relationship. The spirit of engagement is one of collaboration and shared efforts to get to the heart of the matter in anticipation of an amicable restoration process. Key characteristics of someone just as committed to reconciliation as you include being highly: (1) assertive; (2) engaged; and (3) empathetic.

For some, the principles and work around reconciliation will be quick and enjoyable as it confirms what you already know in your heart of hearts about a number of relationships you must address. Many will flow with the process and make the necessary adjustments and move forward with courage and confidence that the people who are meant to be part of their creative and high achieving life will be right there. Others will struggle and hurt through this process. You may even find it frightening as you have never been this raw with emotions because in the past you suppressed them as a coping mechanism to keep you from going insane or breaking down when you had to keep life moving. Because you have never felt this level of uncontrollable emotions, you may be tempted to end the process to once again avoid pain. You will convince yourself that not only is this process not helping, but because of the hurt you are experiencing, you may believe you are actually harming yourself. I believe you are healing as you are finally facing old wounds that keep getting bruised and re-opened because you never allowed them to fully heal in the first place.

As a child I remember falling and getting a big gash on my side. When my family covered up the wound it appeared to be healing to those who saw it from the outside. But I felt pain and discomfort and Grandma had the wisdom to remove the bandage, put some ointment right on the soar and she said, "Don't cover that up. Leave it open and let some air get to it and it will heal faster." I implore you to stop covering up old wounds. Take the bandage off. Allow the healing to begin. Remain open to ideas and activities towards reconciliation that will contribute to your overall quest to live a purpose-driven life.

The work in reconciliation is to discover creative and fruitful strategies for making informed decisions about the relationships you have with genuinely good people in your life. Because you really care about the people who made it onto your list of significant others, take note that the reconciliation process can get messy as you and others discuss events and issues that probably have been avoided up until now. But you owe it to yourself and to the others involved to seek clarity and mutual points of purpose that allow you to move forward as inter-dependents, with each person contributing equally to the uplift and advancement of the other's goals and aspirations. The work sessions in this chapter may prove to be painful and you may find yourself overcome with emotion at time. This is why there is guidance for a "ceasefire." You can stop and begin again as many times as it takes. Keep reminding yourself, however, that reconciliation is a necessary condition for strengthening your soul to ultimately pursue its heart's desire. Use the nine (9) achievement principles in this chapter as guidance for planning your reconciliation process.

PRINCIPLES FOR RECONCILIATION

R	**REALITY**
E	**EMOTIONS**
C	**CEASEFIRE**
O	**OPENNESS**
N	**NEW DEAL**
C	**CHOICES**
I	**INTIMACY**
L	**LESSONS LEARNED**
E	**EMOTIONAL INTELLIGENCE**

Let's Go to Work!

Notes to Self on "Reconciliation"

RECONCILIATION: SUGGESTED PLAYLIST

Song *(Artist)*

1. Reunited *(Peaches and Herb)*

2. I'd Rather have Good Times with You *(Luther Vandross)*

3. We are Family *(Sister Sledge)*

4. Family Reunion *(The OJays)*

5. I Wanna Know what Love is *(Journey)*

6. Let's Stay Together *(Al Green / Tina Turner)*

7. Wind Beneath My Wings *(Bette Midler)*

8. "It's So Hard To Say Goodbye To Yesterday *(Boyz II Men)*

9. I Apologize *(Anita Baker)*

10. Wings of Forgiveness *(India Arie)*

11. Cats in the Cradle *(Harry Chapin)*

12. Better *(Jessica Ready)*

13. Can You Stand the Rain? *(Johnny Gill)*

14. Bridge Over Troubled Waters *(Simon & Garfunkel)*

15. Your Mercy *(Blessed)*

16. My Life *(Mary J. Blige)*

17. Better Days *(Diane Reeves)*

18. Wildflower *(New Birth)*

19. You Survived *(James Fortune and FIYA)*

20. We Could Have Had It All *(Adelle)*

Reality

"The trouble with reality is it is often clouded by social facts and shallow frames that limit your ability and willingness to face and fix a reality that was 'socially constructed' for you, and not by you."

Dr. Quinn Motivates

Reconciliation requires a willingness to face reality. Many of us bury the truth about our current realities as a way to protect significant others for fear of losing what few benefits we may perceive we derive from "keeping secrets." Others avoid reality to escape having to change an environment or relationship that is no longer working for your good. Most under-achieving creative geniuses hide behind a "socially constructed" form of reality that gives them permission to waddle in a toxic cesspool of mediocrity.

Facing reality necessitates ceasing to make excuses for the people who damaged you. Learn to give people and their actions their proper names. For example, she doesn't just need a little help with her bills. She is a chronic mis-manager of her personal finances. He didn't get into a little trouble. He is a convicted felon. She doesn't just drink a little to calm her nerves. She is an alcoholic. He doesn't just get a little upset about certain things. He is a violent hot head. She didn't just make a mistake on the job. The reality of repeated mistakes is that she is intentionally sabotaging her future for fear of success. She is not partaking in retail therapy. She is a full-blown shop-a-holic caving under a mountain of debt. He is not working late to get ahead. He is a workaholic whose self-worth is primarily measured by money. When you can properly name a reality, then you can change it. Otherwise, you are just living a lie in the state of "denial".

Iyanla Vanzant suggests that one of the many values of being in a proverbial valley is it facilitates truth-telling about the reality of your life. She provides 10 dimensions to address in the valley, including: (1) light; (2) understanding; (3) courage; (4) knowledge and wisdom; (5) other people's problems (OPP); (6) comeuppance; (7) purpose and intent; (8) non-resistance; (9) success; and (10) love.

IT'S TIME TO GO TO WORK: "REALITY"

"Since we cannot change reality, let us change the eyes which see reality."
Nikos Kazantzakis

A proverbial valley experience is one of the best places and times to have a place to force a "reality check." I recommend using Iyanla's work on the valleys we encounter in life to guide you through a reality check aimed at telling the truth about: (1) who you really are; (2) how you ended up being someone or something you are not; and (3) how you plan to reconcile those valley experiences that are no longer serving any good and positive purpose in your life. I have reframed Iyanla's conceptualization of valleys into ten (10) questions to guide your reality check.

IYANLA VANZANT'S VALUE IN THE VALLEY WORKPLAN	
WHEN I AM IN THIS VALLEY	**REALITY OF HOW I GOT IN THIS VALLEY**
1. LIGHT	• What lack of knowledge is manifesting as darkness?
2. UNDERSTANDING	• Who am I judging that is serving as a direct reflection of what I am lacking?
3. COURAGE	• What is it that I do not trust about the process of how my life is unfolding?
4. KNOWLEDGE AND WISDOM	• What knowledge and wisdom do I have, but have not been obedient in acting upon?
5. OTHER PEOPLE'S PROBLEMS	• Who in my life do I need to let solve their own life issues?
6. COMEUPPANCE	• What issue am I grappling with that really requires me to take full responsibility for the current state of affairs?
7. PURPOSE AND INTENT	• How have I wandered away from my pursuit of a purpose that I once had clarity on?
8. NON-RESISTANCE	• Who do I need to cooperate with and what needs to happen for either compromise or surrender?
9. SUCCESS	• How have I under-valued my self-worth in ways that are impacting my drive for success?
10. LOVE	• From whom have I withheld unconditional love as a reflection of self-hatred?

EMOTIONS

"We create chronic drama and re-traumatization by wishing that the people in our lives were someone else."
Dr. Quinn Motivates

Our society has sanctioned pain management in such a way that it has become the norm to avoid feelings. Unfortunately, these suppressed feelings are very unhealthy. Shutting down, covering up, redirecting, or numbing feelings produces "dis-ease" and robs us of the ability to heal, as well as empathize with others. Also, remember that pain management regimens can become addictive behaviors even if at first glance they appear "socially acceptable", such as serving others, shopping, or eating to make us feel better when facing a negative emotion. Moreover, extreme emotional mood swings could represent a more severe mental health disorder of bi-polar, which requires clinical care and perhaps medication. In any case, numbing pain can result in addictive habits as a quick response to squash negative emotions.

As you get closer to the root cause of what resulted in the tension, rift, or rupture in the relationship in the first place, the more likely it is that you will experience a range of emotions. The main reason is because we expect optimum creative cooperation, equitable collaboration, and high moral codes of conduct from "social" and "significant" others who may not be emotionally equipped to give us what we expect. There are five (5) different aspects of emotions that tend to cause anxiety and pain. These include fear, shame, guilt, sadness, and anger. Allow yourself to feel the full range of emotions that are part of the reconciliation process and resist the need to numb the pain or shut down to avoid the feelings. You need to get the pain out of you to allow yourself to properly process the emotions. This work is not intellectual or linear by no means because by nature, emotions cloud, confuse, and impair our ability to reason logically.

It's time to go to Work: "Emotions"

"Every day we have plenty of opportunities to get angry, stressed or offended. But what you're doing when you indulge in these negative emotions is giving something outside yourself power over your happiness. You can choose to not let little things upset you."

Joel Osteen

No doubt there are life experiences that rightfully trigger negative emotions. For example, death, depression, economic downturns, and injustice are just a few circumstances where negative emotions might be acceptable responses. Familiarize yourself with how negative emotions impact your life and impair your relationships.

1. *Fear* sets in when there is perceived or real danger, hurt, harm, or pain.

2. *Shame* manifests as feeling bad about who you are or your physical characteristics, and is often rooted in childhood experiences with adult violators, and peer bullying.

3. *Guilt* is feeling bad about something you have done that perhaps caused hurt or harm to yourself or others. Additionally, one can suffer from survivors' guilt as a result of being successful when others in your environment did not fare as well.

4. *Sadness* is associated with feelings of disadvantage, loss, despair, helplessness, and sorrow, often surfacing when we are victimized, abandoned, or rejected by others.

5. *Anger* centers around being upset or outraged based on some form of unfair treatment. Anger can be displayed as an external explosion, while others mask anger through silent resentful behaviors.

In reviewing these typical emotions, it is easy to see how they can set in as seemingly reasonable responses under difficult conditions. The work to be done is to replace these negative emotions with more fruitful responses as follows: (1) Love: build healthy relationships; (2) Joy: rejoice in any situation; (3) Peace: overcome anxiety and conflict; (4) Longsuffering: wait with patience; (5) Gentleness: be kind to one another; (6) Goodness: live generously; (7) Faithfulness: hope for a better future; (8) Meekness: be tender with yourself and others; and (9) Temperance: master one's passions and urges.

CEASEFIRE

"Sometimes the reconciliation process breaks down before there is a breakthrough. Give yourself permission to take a break."

Dr. Quinn Motivates

One of the risks of pursuing reconciliation is that it may touch off a range of emotions from total rejection of your attempts to fierce outrage. When reconciliation efforts unleash years of suppressed abuse, hurt, neglect, and pain, it may be necessary to take an adult time out that I call a "unilateral ceasefire" where someone has to be the "shero." During the ceasefire accept that you have decided to stop the dysfunctional exchanges that are fruitless at that point. However, this doesn't mean that the other person will stop spewing venom and lashing out. Therefore, when you decide in your heart of hearts to pursue a ceasefire, accept that it is a unilateral decision.

A unilateral ceasefire allows you to commit to the spiritual cleansing process known as "surrender" where you release toxic mental and emotional memories associated with the relationship. Surrendering is a very quiet and peaceful process where you allow others their right to tell the story as they experienced it even if the details and facts are fuzzy or outright lies. Surrendering allows you to live through the experience of hearing and resisting the need to respond or retaliate. A commitment to surrender releases you from deep-seated anger, fear, guilt, shame and resentment of all that has transpired over the course of the relationship. The best part of surrendering is being freed from the need to control how the other person sees you and the past you shared.

A very valuable application of the unilateral ceasefire concept is to bring closure. Closure is necessary when you know the other person is either non-committal, too hostile, in denial, or unavailable due to death, abandonment or mental incapacitation. Closure is an independent process where you apply your strength of self-care to bring closure to the unpleasant actions and painful memories and to the extent possible focus on any pleasant parts of the relationship.

IT's TIME TO GO TO WORK: "CEASEFIRE"

"Everything that irritates us about others can lead us to an understanding of ourselves."
Carl Jung

Carl Jung was a Swiss psychiatrist and psychotherapist who founded analytical psychology. As implied in his quote above, a unilateral ceasefire provides the time and space to better understand oneself. Use the questions below to guide you through the very emotional process of determining whether or not a ceasefire is a viable choice based upon a number of factors.

Identify people in your life with whom you have "toxic" or dysfunctional relationships right now. Include people in intimate relationships/sexual partners, family, social, and business/professional.

1. What is the nature of the conflict as I define it?
2. Why is it important for me to resolve it?
3. What are my boundaries and deal breakers in pursuing reconciliation?
4. How can I create a win/win environment?
5. What am I prepared to do if this person rejects reconciliation?

GUIDING PRINCIPLES FOR A UNILATERAL "CEASEFIRE"

1. Trust the process by honoring your alone time to reflect, release, restore, and renew yourself.
2. Accept responsibility for choices you made that contributed to the toxic relationship.
3. Detox of dysfunctional relationships by forgiving and granting grace and mercy as you surrender and release yourself from any strongholds and emotional entanglements.
4. Commit to examine what you learned and need to work on as a result of being in a relationship with this person.
5. Develop coping mechanisms for when you still have to be in the presence of that person during the cease fire.
6. Celebrate and be grateful for the good times and good deeds.
7. Free yourself from being held as an emotional or financial hostage.
8. Write a letter and decide after you complete it whether to keep it as a reminder to avoid going back or to give it to the person for either closure or hopes that a new beginning is on the horizon.

Openness

"Pure openness is the greatest display of freedom because you never know how your truth will be received once you release it into the universe."

Dr. Quinn Motivates

Only a person who is open to a life of transparency and vulnerability is ready to courageously pursue their greatest potential. The idea of openness is predicated on your willingness to reveal your most intimate thoughts without attempting to control how others respond. Begin by opening yourself to telling the truth and hearing the truth no matter how painful. Tell the truth without needing agreement or approval. At the same time, open yourself to hear the truth about how you may have hurt people you really love and desire to have a close relationship with. Openness does not mean you agree with others, but rather it means you are open to listen to their thoughts and feelings.

Another place to explore openness is related to your motives. Let's be honest. We all are motivated to some degree based on the two extremes of self-preservation to meet basic needs and self-actualization to achieve our success goals. However, we encounter problems when we attempt close relationships, but fail to disclose our personal and hidden agendas. The reason why many of us don't achieve optimum levels of functioning in our relationships is because we hide our agendas or we use people to get our personal goals and objectives met at others' expense and in ways that leave them feeling used and violated. Also, be open to hear the possibility that you may not have intentionally set out to use others for your benefit, but somehow the "give and take" became disproportionate and you took more than you gave.

When you are truly living a life of openness you have no secrets. Of course you remain discrete about your lived experiences and use emotional intelligence as a guide for what to share and under what conditions. Many of us stop short of attempting great things because we are afraid that our deepest and darkest secrets will be exposed on some public stage.

It's time to go to Work: "Openness"

"Your perspective on life comes from the cage you were held captive in."
Shannon L. Alder

A key reason people avoid "openness" in general is to avoid exposing negative aspects of "self." According to crisis manager Judy Smith, it is impossible to address adequately crises, conflicts, and chaos that come with the territory of advancing to higher levels of achievement unless you open yourself to the unpleasant areas of your life. I recommend using what she refers to as the "big seven (7)" to make peace with the aspects of "self" that must be addressed in order to live your best life in the most transparent light imaginable. As you work through these seven (7) traits on a path of being more open, continue to ask yourself, "What is the worst that could happen if I open myself to intimate relationships, business partnerships, and innovative strategies for goal attainment?"

JUDY SMITH'S 7 TRAITS FOR ADDRESSING EVERY CRISIS		
	How This Trait Has Negatively Impacted your Life	*What changes need to be made to avoid crisis brought on by this trait?*
1. Ego		
2. Denial		
3. Fear		
4. Ambition		
5. Accommodations		
6. Patience		
7. Indulgence		

Notes to Self on "Openness"

NEW DEAL

"Real relationships will be tested periodically, which serves as a time and space to examine your growth."
Dr. Quinn Motivates

When it comes to reconciliation, the process begins with examining your "dealings" with the person(s) you are considering reconciling with. Typically, you remember "the ideal" when the relationship was fresh and you had high hopes. Then you recall "ordeals" where you focus on the conflicts that may have occurred over time. We sometimes discover that we have experienced a "raw deal" in that we gave more than we got. If we are honest, we open ourselves to the "real deal" that results in truth telling about what this relationship really represents in your life. Acknowledging the real deal brings you to the point of deciding upon a "new deal" or to "no longer deal" with this person.

In preparing to decide on how you will deal with an individual in the future, I recommend spiritualist Don Miquel Ruiz's "The Four Agreements" as guiding principles on how to act and react in ways that create harmony and happiness in your life. The four (4) agreements are: (1) be impeccable with your words; (2) don't take anything personally; (3) don't make assumptions; and (4) always do your best.

It is easy to commit to the four (4) agreements, and incorporate the seven (7) habits into your life. The real work begins in dealing with difficult people who are part of your "built system", thereby forcing some degree of interaction on a regular basis. These difficult individuals are not trying to change because their methods work for them. In the workshop session that follows, take a look at the kinds of difficult people that you must learn to work with even if they do not acknowledge or change their difficult ways.

It's time to go to Work: "New Deal"

"If civilization is to survive, we must cultivate the science of human relationships - the ability of all peoples, of all kinds, to live together, in the same world at peace."

Franklin D. Roosevelt

For the most part, it takes time to work negative, difficult people out of your life, although some people have been known to do abrupt cut-offs. In the meantime, I have adapted Rick Brinkman and Rick Kirschner's work "Dealing with People You Can't Stand" to help you cope with diverse types of difficult people.

AN ADAPTATION OF BRINKMAN AND KIRSCHNER'S METHODOLOGY FOR DEALING WITH DIFFICULT PEOPLE	
DIVERSE TYPES OF DIFFICULT PEOPLE	HOW TO "DEAL" WITH THEM
TOSHA "THE TANK" feels like she has to prove that her opinion is the only right opinion.	• Speak affirmatively from your own point of view and don't let Tosha bully you into accepting her ideas if you really don't agree.
SABRINA "THE SNIPER" will do things to make others look stupid in front of a group of people.	• Call Sabrina out in public on her sneak attacks and tear down of others using concrete examples.
ERICA "THE EXPLODER" lets issues pile up prior to exploding in either a tantrum or melt down.	• Don't take Erica's rage personally because she is generally acting out on past wrongs and hurts.
SONYA "THE SUPER AGREEABLE" wants everyone to love her, so she overloads on activities that bring her admiration.	• Call Sonya out on her inability to complete all that she has committed to do.
CARMEN "THE COMPLAINER" complains about others, however she will never volunteer to lead.	• Acknowledge Carmen, then ignore her unless her complaints include great solutions to build upon.
NATASHA "THE NEGATIVE" is bitter about life in general, and often feels un-empowered.	• Avoid getting drawn into Natasha's negativity as she will drain your energy.
KATRINA "THE KNOW IT ALL" believes everything should be done with high standards.	• Acknowledge Katrina for being smart as she typically has done intense work around the issue at hand.
TAMARA "THE THINK SHE KNOWS IT ALL" wants to be respected by trying to act like she has all the information, but she typically has "bits and pieces," but lacks the big picture perspective.	• Do your own homework and set the record straight when Tamara presents limited information in her quest to be a "Katrina".
INGRID "THE INDECISIVE" believes that until something can be done with perfection she will just not do anything.	• Establish a safe place for Ingrid to open up and share as she is typically quite analytical even if she can't make a decision.
UNISIA "THE UNRESPONSIVE" believes she can control situations by just shutting down.	• Engage Unisia in open-ended questions. Don't feel the need to fill in the silence.

CHOICES

"It takes unprecedented courage to make choices that force others to own their choices."
Dr. Quinn Motivates

Every choice you make has the power to bring you closer to your creative thinking and high achieving goals or driving you further away from that which you truly desire. Each choice that you make no matter how big or small, intentional or unconscious, relevant or irrelevant is tied to your destiny. Even the choice not to choose contributes to shaping your reality in very profound ways. Choices ultimately reflect your character, values, and goals. The revealing truth about choices is that as you ponder your options, you are constantly grappling with two extreme dimensions of yourself. Whether you choose to admit it out loud or not, as you try to manage external impressions of yourself, you constantly weigh the needs of your selfish side against the desire of your compassionate/caring side. If you make choices when you are angry, you are more likely to yield to the selfish and even vindictive side. If you choose from a place of compassion, then the choice tends to serve the greater good for all impacted.

The journey to making responsible choices requires that you bravely become fully aware of the inherent power associated with your good and bad self. This journey involves hard work, heart work, and head work to get to a place where you are making responsible choices the majority of the time. When you operate from a commitment to make responsible choices, you actually take the time to account for all the consequences you put in motion just on your one choice alone. This requires a life-long commitment to place clarity, wisdom, and compassion as priorities in choosing responsibly. This doesn't mean the selfish and vindictive side of you is eliminated. It simply means that you are able to quickly rule out choices to act in selfish and vindictive ways because you fully understand the consequences associated with those choices. When faced with difficult choices in particular, ask yourself, "Once I make this choice, what is it going to create or produce?" Do I really want to create that, and are those consequences I am willing to live with unapologetically?

It's Time to Go to Work: "Choices"

"What you choose, with each action and each thought, is an intention, a quality of consciousness that you bring to your action or your thought."

Gary Zukav

As the concept of "choices" is presented under the theme of reconciliation, the workshop activity below is about choices commonly associated with the process of reconciling relationships that are important to you. I was inspired by spiritual psychologist and author Dr. Grace's work on 10 good choices that empower black women's lives.

DR. QUINN'S STEPS TO RECONCILIATION (AS INSPIRED BY DR. GRACE CORNISH)	
1. Give yourself permission to love your total package	• Unpack all the negative childhood memories and messages that brought you anger, fear, guilt, sadness and shame. Replace that baggage with the total package of a more positive aspect of what you want in relationships.
2. Clarify your relationship values	• Examine the repeated patterns and themes you have made since high school concerning intimate love partners (not sexual per se) and separate the healthy from the unhealthy.
3. Change your relationship with money	• Review all the ways in which you mismanage finances in relation to your relationships. Develop a plan for eliminating dysfunction in your life that cost you the most money.
4. Visualize the endgame associated with your choices	• Determine the extent to which you are willing to live with the consequences of unpopular choices that get you closer to your goal.
5. Separate traumatic events from dramatic episodes	• Define traumatic events as externally-driven experiences. • Define dramatic episodes as the chaos you create in your own life.
6. Trust your intuition	• Learn to trust your intuition when it comes to relationship choices.
7. Be creative in taking calculated chances	• Make responsible relationship choices by calculating the costs and consequences.
8. Address the issues that grieve you	• If there is something that keeps you up at night concerning a particular relationship, put a definitive "decision-day" along with all the possible options on the calendar. On that day, make a decision and stick with it.
9. Rewrite your life's script	• See yourself as the playwright, director, and producer of your future life solely responsible for your life story.
10. Revise the way you pray	• Rely upon spiritual guidance for the choices you must make. Some scripture passages that may calm you during more difficult decisions include: (1) Psalm 51; (2) The Lord's Prayer; (3) The 23rd Psalm; (4) Psalm 142 1-5, Psalm 46; and (5) The Prayer of Jabez.

INTIMACY

"Intimacy begins with being 'into me' because you cannot be fully present for others until you know who you are and what you desire at the very core of your being."

Dr. Quinn Motivates

The research on intimacy provides a glimpse into an area where most creative and high achieving individuals do not fare well. No matter how measured, data indicates that high-profile individuals simply do not have a good track record with intimacy. As I examined the intimate lives of high-profile individuals, I learned that the ones with healthy longevity are characterized by shared values, goals, and genuine support and encouragement for one another to strive unselfishly for excellence with no fear of one outgrowing the other.

The question becomes then how do you increase the likelihood of being able to be successful in an intimate relationship while not compromising on one's quest for higher achievements. The formula for optimizing intimacy is a three-level commitment. First, you must commit to an intimate relationship with the Divine in your life. Second, you must commit to an intimate relationship with yourself. Then you are able to commit to bringing a whole, trusting, and fully present individual to be joined in intimacy with another.

Reconciling an intimate relationship can be the most difficult of all especially if trust has been compromised. The reason so many relationships are broken is because we are socialized to seek a socially desirable and physically compatible mate before we spend the proper time getting to know ourselves. This is why so many can be married for years and never be fulfilled in that union. They survive under rules of domestication and marital civility. However, they fall short of a true spiritual partnership as characterized by intellectual, emotional, experiential, and sexual intimacy. Collectively, these centers of intimacy evolve into love that is defined as a vital source of energy and direction where two people are connected at the head and heart in a way that is supportive of each other's growth.

IT'S TIME TO GO TO WORK: "INTIMACY"

"Solitude is very different from a 'time-out' from our busy lives. Solitude is the very ground from which community grows. Whenever we pray alone, study, read, write, or simply spend quiet time away from the places where we interact with each other directly, we are potentially opened for a deeper intimacy with each other."

Henri Nouwen

Intimacy with the Divine. For reconciliation with the Divine, I recommend using American Christian author Stormie Omartian's workbook and journal titled "Lord, I want to Be Whole." In her work she details seven (7) steps for pursuing wholeness with the Divine that include: (1) release the past; (2) live in obedience; (3) find deliverance; (4) seek total restoration; (5) receive God's gifts; (6) reject pitfalls; and (7) stand strong.

Intimacy with Self. For reconciliation with self, I recommend working through relationships coach Debrena Jackson Gandy's 101 sacred principles for making joy real in your life as outlined in her book "All the Joy You Can Stand." Select principles from Gandy's work that are directly related to intimacy include: (1) learn self-love; (2) free up energy in your life; (3) define yourself; (4) know the source of your personal power; (5) tell the truth; (6) purge and cleanse; (7) create intimacy with sister friends; (8) pray and meditate; (9) rewrite the script; and (10) free your creative genius.

Intimacy with a Significant Other. For reconciling with a significant other, I recommend working through relationship counselor and author Dr. Gary Chapman's work on "The Five Love Languages". The Five Love Languages include: (1) words of affirmation; (2) quality time, (3) receiving gifts; (4) acts of service; and (5) physical touch.

Lessons in Living

"You will repeat life's tests until you finally learn what each lesson is responsible for teaching you. Please don't flunk the final exam."

Dr. Quinn Motivates

One of the reasons why we tend to repeat negative historical patterns in our lives is because we block out the need to process them as lessons by which to live. As most of our lessons learned center on some intimate relationship, I cringe at the Beyoncé song titled "To the Left." This is the story of our lives. As she is putting out the old, she is affirming that in just one minute she is going to be back in the same type of situation. The issue is we don't do the work to process bad relationships adequately before entering into the next potentially unhealthy arrangement. You have to take time to figure out the purpose of the continued challenges and obstacles around relationships. There are some universal lessons learned that include the need to: (1) own your power to choose or continue to be reactionary; (2) be fully present and accountable for all areas of your life; and (3) accept responsibility for the changes that must be made that bring you closer to the life you desire.

4 DIMENSIONS OF LEARNING FROM LESSONS IN LIFE

1. *Past enthusiasm.* What are those experiences that ignite positive energy and inspire you to want to be greater?

2. *Painful exposure.* What past experiences were embarrassing and perhaps triggered a range of negative emotions such as anger, guilt, sadness, shame, or humiliation?

3. *Present environment.* What is my current set of experiences trying to teach me? Am I repeating hurtful situations because I failed to apply past opportunities to learn?

4. *Perspective on expectations.* How have lessons I have learned in life shaped my perspective on what is possible for me to achieve in this life time?

IT'S TIME TO GO TO WORK: "LESSONS IN LIVING"

"On a spiritual level, we chose to be here at this time and place because we have lessons to learn and contributions to make. We are here to transform ourselves and, in so doing, transform our world.

Susan L. Taylor

Here is a structured process for working through some of life's toughest lessons. These are in the form of questions because you have to answer them for yourself.

DR. QUINN'S METHODOLOGY FOR IDENTIFYING "LESSONS IN LIVING"

1. **RAISE YOUR LEVEL OF CONSCIOUSNESS.** What knowledge and information do I need to access in order to make better decisions in the future?

2. **RELEASE NEGATIVE EMOTIONS.** How did this experience impact me emotionally and what is my plan of action to address the negative emotions stemming from this experience?

3. **CONDUCT AN EXECUTIVE SESSION WITH YOURSELF.** Am I able to step outside of myself and critique my own actions in terms of the role I played in allowing the experience to continue? What are my values and bottom-line and how will I make better choices because of my clarity on standards?

4. **ASSESS KEY ENVIRONMENTS.** How did various environments within which I live, work, play, and worship impact and influence the experience in question?

5. **FREE YOURSELF FROM UNHEALTHY PEOPLE.** What people do I need to limit or eliminate my interactions with as they contributed directly or indirectly to the experience?

6. **NURTURE HEALTHY RELATIONSHIPS.** What people were supportive during the experience even if I couldn't appreciate it at the time?

7. **IDENTIFY POSITIVE ALTERNATIVE BEHAVIORS.** What am I going to do differently to avoid getting into similar situations in the future?

8. **DEVELOP A PLAN FOR BEHAVIOR REINFORCEMENT.** How will I positively reward myself in the future for taking positive steps to avoid harmful experiences?

9. **FREE YOURSELF FROM GENERATIONAL BONDAGE.** What unresolved issues from my past contribute to my continuing to make unhealthy decisions?

10. **ENGAGE IN HEALTHY ACTIVITIES.** What can I do physically and socially to help me avoid triggers that may cause me to relapse to the old ways of thinking, doing, and selecting that ultimately netted less than positive results in my life?

NOTES TO SELF ON "LESSONS IN LIVING"

Emotional Intelligence

"The essence of emotional intelligence is that hard questions require heart answers and heart questions require hard answers."
Dr. Quinn Motivates

Emotional intelligence is fundamental to the reconciliation process. At the heart of emotional intelligence is a genuine effort to see the world from the viewpoint of others. Understanding the conditions shaping another's decision-making is the essence of empathy. You are constantly asking yourself, "What would I have done under the same circumstances and constraints?" This doesn't mean you agree with the person's actions, especially if they caused others harm, but rather you learn to appreciate the factors that may have driven this person to be the way they are and act the way they do.

A sincere degree of empathy manifests in your communications where you resist the need to react or respond when hearing the perspective of others. Empathic listening sends a message that you value the relationship enough to hear what the other person has to say uninterruptedly. To get to this level of authentic empathy requires work. This work begins with deconstructing the concept of emotional intelligence. Enhancing your skills and tools in the area of emotional intelligence is what I call bridging the gap between what happens in your head and what you feel in your heart.

Emotional intelligence results in a comprehensive perspective on how to reconcile what is happening in one's head and one's heart. When there is a lack of head and heart coordination, one is said to be "emotionally ignorant." Emotionally ignorant invividuals believe that treating everyone the same yields similar results. They operate out of a spirit of fairness and justice that takes precedent over grace and mercy. The emotionally ignorant are not "wrong" per se' in being more head strong. However, they are less concerned with the potential traumatization they could trigger when rigidly holding to what is "right."

It's Time to Go to Work: "Emotional Intelligence"

"Emotional intelligence begins to develop in the earliest years. All the small exchanges children have with their parents, teachers, and with each other carry emotional messages."

Daniel Goleman

The model for emotional intelligence was introduced by author, psychologist, and science journalist Daniel Goleman, and includes five (5) elements associated with having a high degree of emotional intelligence. Review these areas and think about your current strengths and challenges.

DANIEL GOLEMAN'S CORE ELEMENTS OF EMOTIONAL INTELLIGENCE			
CORE AREAS	DEFINITION	CURRENT STRENGTHS	CHALLENGES
1. SELF-AWARENESS	• the ability to know one's emotions, strengths, weaknesses, drives, values and goals and recognize their impact on others while using gut feelings to guide decisions		
2. SELF-REGULATION	• involves controlling or redirecting one's disruptive emotions and impulses and adapting to changing circumstances		
3. SOCIAL SKILL	• managing relationships to move people in the desired direction		
4. EMPATHY	• considering other people's feelings especially when making decisions		
5. MOTIVATION	• being driven to achieve for the sake of achievement		

NOTES TO SELF ON "EMOTIONAL INTELLIGENCE"

CONFIRMATION

"the act of increasing your confidence in the purpose for your life."

"Confirmation is not some mystically deep process requiring intense analytical work, but rather it is a product of embodying the confidence to act upon what is being confirmed as you internalize that which you perceive to be true about what you are capable of accomplishing in this life time."

Dr. Quinn Motivates

We all have gifts and talents God provided to achieve a unique life purpose. The significance of confirmation is to serve as a catalyst to take bold, confident strides in pursuing your purpose-driven life. The difficulty comes in seeking clarity on how best to utilize some combination of gifts and talents. The confirmation process is even more complicated if our everyday lives are completely opposite from what our heart is telling us is our "calling." What I know from my work with gifted and talented people is that you have had more than enough encounters, experiences, ideas, intuition, signals, signs, and thoughts that all work together as "confirmation." The problem is fear of the responsibility for being accountable for what you do with your gifts and talents. In order to calm this fear, you have to shift your "perception" and "perspectives" as you answer the questions: (1) what on earth am I here to accomplish?; and (2) what is my capacity for fully embracing that which I can accomplish?

PERCEPTIONS AND PERSPECTIVES

In its simplest form, perception is what you internalize as you experience the world around you; whereas perspective is gained by your interaction with others who share the world with you. Among things, perceptions and perspectives collectively confirm that which you think is possible. Over time, continued points of perceptions and perspectives provide clarity and courage in a way that replaces doubt and fear related to what on earth you are here to do.

Confirmation is enhanced as you reconcile clarity that comes from within (perception) and clarity that comes from interacting with the world in which you operate (perspective). Clarity within these two phenomena clears the way for your head and heart to be fully dedicated to pursue your purpose. In this way, confirmation stimulates the head and the heart in ways that allow you to forge ahead knowing that you are on the right track. As you review how perceptions and perspectives contribute to the confirmation process, note the relative weight of my writings on these two concepts. I am sending a strong message that more time should be spent on gaining clarity from the inside out (perceptions) in comparison to focusing on the world out there (perspectives of others).

The role of "perception" in the confirmation process. Perception is about becoming more conscious of your experiences and encounters in ways that contribute to confirming that which you are uniquely designed to create or achieve. The key to building your courage to act upon that which you perceive, is to become intensely aware of the world around you. Environmental awareness includes how you use your five (5) senses (hearing, sight, smell, taste and touch) to interact with people, places, and things. As you experience the world around you, you encounter people and situations that serve as "environmental stimuli." Your continued interaction with select external stimulation is key to how you see and respond to the world. As you start to make sense of the many points of perception that at first glance may seem unrelated, you begin to see patterns, re-occurrences, and trends that present as "confirmation" if you are willing to pay attention.

The role of "perspective" in the confirmation process. Perspective differs slightly from perception in that perspective entails a more complex understanding of how you see the world and how individuals in the world see you. As it relates to confirmation, the perspectives of others about what you are capable of achieving or creating impacts you in several ways. First, not all perspectives from others about you are positive and supportive. Second, whether good or bad, people provide their perspectives about your life's endeavors even when you didn't ask to be engaged. Third, imbedded in others' diverse perspectives and impressions are viewpoints that you may want to consider as you assess your capabilities and potential.

When I was seeking clarity on the purpose for my life, those I encountered shared their perspectives that I was "playing life too small."   I heard this from people who had never met each other, as well as those who have been in my life in different points in time and in different environments. Even though my resume' is filled with experiences that on its face signal a woman living up to her full potential, I always sensed that I could achieve more. At the same time, I felt guilty for wanting more until I stumbled upon the biblical truth that "to whom much is given much is required." This put my multiple and diverse gifts, enthusiasm, expertise, knowledge, passion, skills, and talents into perspective. As I made the conscious decision to bring my full self to the forefront, I embraced the potential of my work at national and international spheres of influence. As I shifted from "local girl does good" to "Dr. Quinn Motivates" I can look back and see how every encounter and experience served as confirmation. I also learned that certain people were not ready for my brand of motivation as understanding what doesn't work is equally as important in the confirmation process. It is my desire that you commit to the vulnerable, and sometimes painful process of getting clarity via perception and perspective on what you are capable of achieving.

When it's all said and done the confirmation process results in courage and confidence to pursue that which you come to firmly believe you are capable of achieving. The end-product of "confirmation" is that it bridges the gap between clarity, competence, capability, courage, and confidence. The kind of courage and confidence that comes with confirmation is not easily shaken even when plans go awry. You simply trust that you have the strength to cope with challenges as they present themselves throughout your creative process. Without continued confirmation it is easy to lose sight of a creative dream that in its execution will transform life as you know it in exchange for what is practical. Continued confirmation at key twists and turns in the process of high achievement increases your confidence and commitment to embrace "outside-the-box" thinking and seemingly radical actions.

Over time, you come to accept thinking and acting in extraordinary ways as your new normal. You are no longer afraid of the special gifts and strengths that you know you have. This is why it is so important that you guard against people questioning the way you think and move. To avoid being caught off guard by trivial information and "trifling" people in your pursuit, you must remain committed to building your wisdom and understanding of what is required of you with the gifts and talents you have. This level of confirmation assures that you are no longer afraid of the unique and special strength you possess to achieve extraordinary results. In this chapter, I present seven (7) of the *40 achievement principles* related to confirming your life's purpose.

PRINCIPLES FOR CONFIRMATION	
C	CALLING
O	OPEN-MINDED AND OPEN-HEARTED
N	NATURAL AND SUPERNATURAL STRENGTH
F	FORTITUDE
I	IMAGINATION
R	RECLAMATION
M	MOMENTUM

Let's Go to Work!

CONFIRMATION: SUGGESTED PLAYLIST

Song *(Artist)*

1. "My Mind Is Made Up" *(Rev. Milton Brunson & Thompson Community Singers)*

2. "Go Get It" *(Mary Mary)*

3. "I Believe I Can Fly" *(R. Kelly)*

4. "I Believe" *(Fantasia)*

5. "If You Believe" *(Dee Dee Bridgewater/The Wiz Soundtrack)*

6. I Can See Clearly Now *(Johnny Nash)*

7. The Blessings of Abraham *(Donald Lawrence and the Tri-City Singers)*

8. Speak to my Heart *(Donnie McClurkin)*

9. Order my Steps *(GMWA Women of Worship / Brooklyn Tabernacle Choir)*

10. Imagine Me *(Kirk Franklin)*

11. The Gift *(Donald Lawrence & Company)*

12. Don't Stop Believin' *(Journey)*

13. Never Give Up On A Dream *(Rod Stewart)*

14. Shake Yourself Loose *(Vickie Winans)*

15. His Eye is on the Sparrow *(Lauryn Hill; Tonya Blount/Sister Act 2 Soundtrack)*
    (Bubbling Brown Sugar Soundtrack)
    (The Mississippi Children's Choir)

16. Encourage Yourself *(Donald Lawrence and the Tri-City Singers)*

17. I Need you Now *(Smokie Norful)*

18. Stand *(Donnie McClurkin)*

19. For Every Mountain *(Kurt Carr & The Kurt Carr Singers)*

20. Bless Me: Prayer of Jabez *(Donald Lawrence and the Tri-City Singers)*

CALLING

"Talent and skills can be developed, but a calling comes from the Divine in the form of a gift. Therefore, I am convinced that all God's children are gifted."
Dr. Quinn Motivates

Your potential for creative thinking and high achieving is maximized when there is confirmation and clarity that you are moving in the right direction. This process of confirming your calling ultimately gives way to a purpose-driven life where you are thought to be aligning closely to that which you believe you have been "called" to do in this lifetime. An astonishing observation of one deemed to be walking in their "calling" is that what appears to the rest of the world as an effortless performance or flawless execution is in fact a confidence in their gifts, skills, and talents that is not easily explained or replicated.

KEY DIMENSIONS OF A CALLING

GIFT: What you do well or with little effort in comparison to others

SKILLS: What you learned how to do that is typically technical or routine

TALENT: What you do well in the natural, and perfect with practice

The best example is Oprah Winfrey's sincere belief that her calling is simply "to teach." Clearly she did not choose the path of a traditional educator; however her life's work is filled with creative ways to provide her audience with "teachable moments" and "experiential learning experiences." Creative thinking allowed Oprah to redefine what is meant by "classroom" and she defied all tradition in what a curriculum of study looks like. Instead she used the world of journalism stretched in many paths to take people on a journey of self-discovery. I am constantly asked, "How can I be sure that this is my true calling?" In examining Oprah's creative approach I developed a formula for what it means to confirm one's life's calling. Here are the key components for examining whether or not you are acting and living in ways that are consistent with the calling for your life: (1) purpose; (2) personal; (3) passion; (4) preparation; (5) people and partnerships; (6) plan and process); (7) path; (8) pursuit; (9) provision; and (10) performance.

It's Time to Go to Work: "Calling"

"I believe that God has put gifts and talents and ability on the inside of every one of us. When you develop that and you believe in yourself and you believe that you're a person of influence and a person of purpose, I believe you can rise up out of any situation."

Joel Osteen

Use the template below to help you clarify the complex components associated with identifying your life's calling.

DR. QUINN'S 10-POINTS FOR CLARIFYING YOUR CALLING	
KEY COMPONENTS	**QUESTIONS TO BRING CLARITY**
1. PURPOSE	• What are you seeking to accomplish?
2. PERSONAL	• Why do you want to accomplish this particular goal?
3. PASSION	• To what degree do you genuinely enjoy the work involved in achieving this goal?
4. PREPARATION	• How have you developed your gifts and talents through skills-building, knowledge enhancement, and professional and personal growth and development?
5. PEOPLE AND PARTNERSHIPS	• Who are the people and partners you envision being part of your purpose-driven life and under what conditions?
6. PLAN AND PROCESS	• What are your strategies, tactics, and action plans for achieving your overall purpose?
7. PATH	• In what direction will you move in your pursuit of purpose?
8. PURSUIT	• What are your indicators that you are moving in the right direction towards your pursuit?
9. PROVISION	• What resources have been entrusted to you to achieve your purpose?
10. PERFORMANCE	• How will you measure your performance towards accomplishing your goal?

NOTES TO SELF ON "CALLING"

Open-minded and Open-hearted

"Leave your mind and heart open to new beginnings with previously explored ideas and old acquaintances."
Dr. Quinn Motivates

Once your calling is clarified, you must open your heart and mind to new possibilities about how to pursue your life's purpose. In essence, be firm on the calling, but flexible on strategies to pursue it. This blend of firmness and flexibility requires a degree of openness that begins with an understanding that everything in your comfort zone is free game for change. Below are five (5) areas to consider opening yourself for change.

1. *Open to exploring a world beyond your normal.* To what extent are you open to explore a world that results in creating a new "normal"? A deeper exploration of the world opens you to continued possibilities.

2. *Open to a change in environments.* To what extent are you willing to change jobs, or cities to increase your capacity for peak performance? A change in physical environment leads to fresh perspectives.

3. *Open to changes in relationships.* Are you ready for sincere dialogue with significant others about who you really are? The potential for change occurs when you share that which you desire to be, and your intent to become it with or without the support of significant others.

4. *Open to a change in the way you manage money.* When it comes to money, are you using it as an asset to achieve your greatest aspirations; or are you misusing money as a way to maintain your current level of comfort? You will need to open yourself to examining your relationship with money either as a (1) barrier to or (2) facilitator for changing your life.

5. *Open to criticism and feedback.* Are you open to critical feedback? Position yourself to have a thick enough skin to consider new ideas and listen to others with an open mind even when the communicator is less charismatic and nurturing when compared to those you normally seek out to provide feedback and coaching.

IT'S TIME TO GO TO WORK: "OPEN-MINDED & OPEN-HEARTED"

"And Jabez called on the God of Israel, saying, Oh that thou wouldest bless me indeed, and enlarge my coast, and that thine hand might be with me, and that thou wouldest keep me from evil, that it may not grieve me! And God granted him that which he requested."
1 Chronicles 4:10

If you are one of those people that gravitate towards structure and consistency, you may find it more difficult to practice the concept of "openness." When you have closed off change for longer periods of time, the process of opening one's mind and heart may seem impractical, and even impossible. What you are really experiencing is resisting the potential for being viewed as weak, vulnerable, or unfocused during the process of opening yourself up for change. It is true that people with open minds and hearts are at greater risk for being taken advantage of. Over time however, the strengths of openness outweigh the risks. Use the template below to identify what you can gain from being open-minded and open-hearted in key areas.

DR. QUINN'S CORE AREAS FOR AN OPEN-MIND AND OPEN-HEART			
	RESULTS I DESIRE IF I OPEN MY HEART AND MIND IN THIS AREA	THINGS I FEAR MIGHT HAPPEN IF I OPEN MYSELF TO CHANGE IN THIS AREA	CONCRETE STEPS I AM WILLING TO TAKE TO OPEN MYSELF IN THIS SPECIFIC AREA
1. OPEN TO EXPLORING A WORLD BEYOND YOUR NORMAL			
2. OPEN TO A CHANGE IN ENVIRONMENTS			
3. OPEN TO CHANGES IN RELATIONSHIPS			
4. OPEN TO A CHANGE IN THE WAY YOU MANAGE MONEY			
5. OPEN TO CRITICISM AND FEEDBACK			

NOTES TO SELF ON "OPEN-MINDED AND OPEN-HEARTED"

NATURAL AND SUPERNATURAL STRENGTH

"Your gifts from God come with the strength to show up in the world as the gifted child you are."

Dr. Quinn Motivates

Confirmation is the by-product of two (2) phenomena: (1) natural and (2) supernatural. Confirmation from a natural standpoint represents a combination of one's God-given gifts and raw talent, as well as acquired skills and knowledge. Supernatural strength refers to Divine power that amplifies one's natural ability and potential. The difficulty in reconciling that supernatural strength works from the inside out. However in the word in which we live, people want to see outward expressions and symbols of a confirmed calling on one's life. This may result in unprecedented pressures to produce tangible results prematurely.

When there is balance between natural and supernatural strength one is said to be operating with a "zeal" and "zest" for goal pursuit. Having zeal and zest for life allows you to give your all to your pursuit. Zeal and zest ignite as twin fires in the belly illuminating as you perform even the most mundane tasks with passion. When others give up, or give in, you are able to keep going because zeal and zest fuel your faith in the future. A confirmed calling in the natural and supernatural provides a confidence that resonate in the spirit as a belief that you can do all things through supernatural strength that emboldens and empowers your natural efforts.

Natural and supernatural strength manifests as "awe" where others have a deep respect and reverence for the final results. However, the process of how natural and supernatural work together for a particular person's confirmation of life's purpose is not repeatable for others. This is why it is important for each person to do the work to determine her unique potential through combining natural and supernatural strength. When your calling is confirmed through natural and supernatural strength you become resilient. Resilience is the strength of spirit to recover from adversity.

It's Time to Go to Work: "Natural & Supernatural Strength"

"Our potential for fruitful living is great because Jesus is our source. The fact that God is our caretaker and owner adds to that potential."
John C. Maxwell

Supernatural strength is most effective when it coexists with a commitment to the fruits of the spirit as guidance for character and integrity. Review the nine (9) fruits of the spirit within the context of your gifts and talents. Do the work to apply the spiritual fruits in your life as you pursue greatness.

TRASK AND GOODALL'S CONCEPTUALIZATION OF THE FRUITS OF THE SPIRIT
Love: (Seek healthy relationships)
• Replace old relationship paradigms with characteristics grounded in equity, mutuality of purpose, and commitment to uplift and inspire an intimate other.
Joy: (Rejoice in any situation)
• Develop a serene awareness of God's strength and protection under all circumstances.
Peace: (Overcome anxiety and conflict)
• Submit to rest in a real relationship with God.
Patience: (Learn how to wait)
• Be willing to suffer long and endure persecution for that which you desire.
Goodness: (Learn to live generously)
• Strive for moral excellence as exemplified in your character and conduct.
Kindness: (Reach out to others)
• Practice goodness by helping others without expecting anything in return.
Faithfulness: (The foundation of true friendship)
• Resolve to fulfill commitments and promises.
Gentleness: (The strength of being tender)
• Balance your strengths with a peaceful disposition that allows you to present as firm, yet fair.
Self-control: (Master your passions)
• Control your temper and display discipline when your flesh is tested in diverse ways along your pursuit.

Fortitude

"The formula for fortitude is to pray, plan, press, and repeat this process often."
Dr. Quinn Motivates

Fortitude is a necessary display of strength and resolve to achieve against the odds. Once you get moving in the right direction towards maximizing your achievements, expect roadblocks and obstacles. Nothing bothers me more than an individual who fails to plan than one who doesn't have a back-up or contingency plan. The essence of fortitude is planning for victory, yet bracing for conflict, confusion, and controversy as normal evils in your pursuit.

The further along the pursuit you go, the more fortitude you need to clear narrow paths. Fortitude allows you to connect deeply with your desire that you will do whatever it takes without compromising your character and integrity to overcome seemingly insurmountable barriers. Without fortitude you will fold at the first sign of pressure or discomfort. With fortitude, you persist, find a way, figure it out, but what you don't do is fold under pressure. Here are the keys to pursuing your goals with a spirit of fortitude:

1. Plan and prepare thoroughly with clearly defined goals and objectives.
2. Complete every task, resource, and critical path provided to achieve your goals.
3. Make friends with fear and welcome it in any form as it manifests along your pursuit of purpose.
4. Set "decision days" to resolve issues firmly and finitely that conflict with your values and goals.
5. When you experience setbacks, throw a "2-minute" pity party, then switch to an empowerment party.
6. Have a back-up plan for quick recalibration.
7. Resolve the fight with the "inner-me."
8. Focus your energy on the future.
9. Always act with character and integrity.
10. Endure hardships with patience and perseverance.

It's time to go to Work: "Fortitude"

"Wanting something is not enough. You must hunger for it. Your motivation must be absolutely compelling in order to overcome the obstacles that will invariably come your way."

Les Brown

The "fortitude" questionnaire

What do you want and how badly do you want it?

Your answers to this question and the ones below in my "Fortitude Questionnaire" will determine the degree to which you are hungry enough to pursue your goals and aspirations with a spirit of fortitude to press forward with character and integrity.

DR. QUINN'S FORTITUDE QUESTIONNAIRE:
What do you want and how bad do you want it?

1. What do you really want?

2. Why do you think you what it?

3. What are you willing to do to obtain it?

4. Why haven't you obtained it already?

5. For how long have you wanted to achieve this particular thing?

6. If you had a choice, what course of action would you take to get it?

7. What messages have you received from others related to achieving this thing?

8. What gets in your way on a daily basis and hinders you from your goal?

9. What is your biggest fear about that?

10. What are 3 steps you can take within the next 21 days to achieve your goal?

11. What are the deal breakers in your pursuit?

12. What "pet projects" are masquerading as progress towards your ultimate desires?

13. Why are you spending time on those pet projects?

14. What is the most frustrating thing about your life right now?

15. What would it take to eliminate those frustrations?

16. What are your unique skills, talents, or gifts that are under-utilized?

17. What would it take for you to utilize all of your potential?

18. Where do you want to be in 5 years?

19. What is your game plan for getting there?

20. What will be your legacy?

IMAGINATION

"You cannot create anything without a vibrant child-like imagination."
Dr. Quinn Motivates

A core component of a confirmed calling is using your imagination to think beyond where you begin. Imagination unlocks creativity about how you get to the end result. Imagination is the sum total of all that has inspired you to visualize a whole new world of potential and possibility. A vibrant imagination results in: (1) solving old problems in new ways; (2) discovering hidden or buried talents; (3) relying upon intuition with increased confidence; (4) bringing forth suppressed ideas that defy logic; and (5) an increasing curiosity and exploratory nature. When you really reflect upon it, every original thought and new thing in our universe sprung forth from some courageous mind willing to defy logic and embrace imagination. More precisely, all the products, services, movies, TV shows, songs, and even dances have one thing in common: Someone vowed to do the work involved in turning a "thought" into a "thing."

A vibrant imagination gives you permission to revive your mind in any situation, environment, and under any conditions. In fact, the best remedy for addressing a mid-life crisis is to use your imagination to reinvent yourself. Many of us are frightened by the kinds of ideas that come into our minds because we just can't imagine how to get that idea from a concept to a concrete thing. So those thoughts remain imbedded in us as a figment of our imagination. We never stop thinking about the possibility, however we just find a way to get busy with life and avoid putting our gifts and talents to the test to give our imagination life. The work that must be done is to apply child-like principles of imagination as a viable strategy for turning thoughts into things. If you have wondered well away from your calling, the last thing you need right now is logic. What you need is a child-like imagination to stir up your enthusiasm to look beyond immediate obstacles and circumstances. Imagine that!

It's time to go to Work: "Imagination"

"I only hope that we don't lose sight of one thing - that it was all started by a mouse."
Walt Disney

Authentic imagination relies very little on formal instructions and directions. Here are some effective strategies for getting adults to indulge in the spirit of imagination.

1. *Keep a "journey" notebook.* Keep a notebook that is simple and playful where you use colorful pens to journal your ideas about your future. Think of it as an idea jotter and not a planner, organizer, or agenda.

2. *Act out your alter ego.* Dress the part and assume the role of some profession or character that gives you energy.

3. *Give your inner-child permission to play.* Play child-age games and participate in activities typically reserved for kids ten (10) and under.

4. *Paint, draw, scribble.* Use vibrant colors and music in the background.

5. *Develop a vision board.* Paste pictures of the things you imagine for your life beyond material possessions.

6. *Develop a vision statement.* Your vision board should result in a vision statement that connects all that you imagine in a coherent sentence. As it is future-oriented, your vision statement includes what it is you want to become in this life time that is legendary.

Use my perspective on "VISION" to help you think through the process of preparing a "vision board" and an accommodating "vision statement" as a constant reminder of that which you wish to create in your life.

DR. QUINN'S PERSPECTIVE ON "VISION"		
V	VISUALIZE VICTORY	Begin with the end game in mind.
I	INSIGHTFUL IMAGING	Identify what a successful you looks like
S	STRATEGIES FOR SUCCESS	Select strategies that challenge you
I	INNOVATIVE IDEAS	Get out of the box
O	OWN YOUR DREAMS	Don't let the odds and obstacles intimidate you
N	NO LIMITS	Think beyond your "right now"

Reclamation

"If you have experienced failure by sabotaging, procrastinating, neglecting, and avoiding your dream, it is time to reclaim it."

Dr. Quinn Motivates

In the process of confirming your calling, you will discover that you have made a lot of excuses in this life time as to why you are not where you should be. Now is the time to stop giving power to delays and disappointments through very meticulously crafted explanations that minimize the fact that you have not done what you set out to do. Instead, do the work to reclaim that which will bring you fulfillment. Simply find a way to commit to doing it once and for all. Be clear that encounters of resistance are signs that you are pushing past the point of no return to reclaim that which is meaningful to you. This time, as you reclaim and recommit, before you quit or delay again, have a game plan in place for recognizing issues that present to derail you.

The reclamation process is about unlocking buried treasures of ambition locked up in your soul. Revisit the excuses that you have used to prevent yourself from excelling and achieving your dreams. Start by eliminating the self-imposed boundaries and limitations. In the next chapter you will have an opportunity to work on reclaiming important relationships. However, a prerequisite is to engage in alone time so you can explore how being entangled in other people's problems moved you further way from your own goals and objectives. This doesn't make you selfish. It helps you remove anything that looks like co-dependency from your life.

Reclaim your heart's desire. Never give up on pursuing the thing you were created to do and the person you really want to be. Re-inventing yourself really is about embracing your authentic self that got lost along the journey as you made what seemed like the best choice at a particular time in your life. At that time you lacked appropriate insight and foresight to know that life would have worked out much better had you stayed the course of your calling despite struggles and obstacles.

It's Time to Go to Work: "Reclamation"

"One of the problems of today's society is that people don't want to make commitments. Why? Because to commit yourself to a goal means you must close the door on all other options. The committed person leaves no alternative. She eliminates all other options."

Dr. Robert A. Schuller

The confirmation process includes reclaiming dreams and goals that have been discarded for various reasons. Use the table below to jumpstart your reclamation. This exercise is particularly helpful for those who put their own aspirations on hold to support others.

DR. QUINN'S 12 STEPS TO RECLAMING YOUR LIFE	
STEPS	**STRATEGY FOR RECLAMATION**
1. GET ENTHUSIASTIC	
2. LET LOVE LIBERATE YOU	
3. RELY UPON DIVINE POWER FOR STRENGTH	
4. HONOR YOUR RIGHT TO MAKE A DIFFERENT CHOICE	
5. UNCOVER YOUR HIDDEN TREASURES	
6. HANDLE YOUR HASSLES HEAD ON	
7. BECOME A POSSIBILITY THINKER	
8. PRAY AND MEDITATE	
9. GROW YOUR FAITH	
10. OPEN DOORS	
11. PRACTICE WHAT YOU THINK	
12. PURSUE YOUR PURPOSE	

NOTES TO SELF ON "RECLAMATION"

Momentum

"Momentum starts with recognizing and seizing the moment, but you have to be smart enough to know the difference between a minute and a moment."

Dr. Quinn Motivates

Every creative thinker and high achiever has a God-breathed calling on their lives. Once you work through the process of confirming your calling, it is imperative that you get moving! Not only must you get moving, but you must develop an obstacle-proof plan to keep moving in the direction of fulfilling the mission attached to your calling. This is called gaining and maintaining momentum. Even baby steps are acceptable at the beginning of your movement into your calling.

Momentum is very much a discussion about motivation. In this case a confirmed calling serves as the motivation to encourage you to take the first steps. The first step is simply creating a clear vision of where you want to end up. However, because many of us have gone in the wrong direction for a long period of time, we have to spend time turning around, stopping what isn't working, and silencing unnecessary noise.

Momentum is created and maintained by creating a series of action steps. The key is to figure out how to keep going when you encounter challenges and roadblocks. Ways to outmaneuver obstacles include identifying what you believe to be the core elements of your calling, breaking down old systems, and eliminating unhealthy habits that are not consistent with your calling. Also, insert yourself into circles of kindred spirits with similar callings. Develop an unshakeable plan for moving forward. As you are in motion, do a "momentum" check that includes answering: "Am I progressing in the right direction?" "Am I doing the right things?" "Am I doing things right?" The key is to remain in motion to the extent possible by staying focused on what you desire, keeping the faith, and showing up ready to move FORWARD - mentally, spiritually, and literally! This is your cyber life coach screaming *let go! and let's go!*

IT'S TIME TO GO TO WORK: "MOMENTUM"

"What simple action could you take today to produce a new momentum toward success in your life?"
Tony Robbins

When it comes to higher levels of achievement, gaining and maintaining momentum is paramount. In my cursory study of physics, I have identified vocabulary words that help you understand how key aspects of "momentum" are related to human behavior. Answer these questions within the context of giving your higher aspiration goals everything you have to achieve it.

DR. QUINN'S MOMENTUM QUESTIONNAIRE	
ASSESSING YOUR PLAN FOR GAINING AND MAINTAINING MOMENTUM	
FOCUS	What has your attention or what are you attracted to that is contributing positively or negatively to your quest to gain and maintain momentum towards achieving your goal?
WEIGHT	How are you going to get your weight up as a way to convert the "fat" in your life to "muscle"?
SPEED	How fast do you want to pursue your goal?
DIRECTION	In what direction do you need to be moving?
MAGNITUDE	How big or large do you see yourself being?
EXTERNAL FORCES	What in the universe is serving as an externally-driven force of motivation towards your goal-attainment?
ENERGY	What is serving as fuel or energy in your life?
MOTIVATION	Why do you keep going?
MOTION	Once you get moving, what is your game plan to keep moving? *(As you respond to this question, remember the law of inertia: a body at rest tends to stay at rest; a body in motion tends to stay in motion.)*
TRANSFORMATION	What is your end game for completing your life's mission?

TRANSFORMATION
"The process of undergoing dramatic change in one or more areas of life"

"Everyone is on their own journey and if you are lucky you get some good friends to join you for a short walk on your way to your destiny."

Dr. Quinn Motivates

Transformation is about creating your most attractive vision of the future, and removing any barriers to achieving it. No matter your goal or aspiration, transformation happens in four (4) distinct, but connected shifts:

1. A shift in desire *(heart)*
2. A shift in thinking *(head)*
3. A shift in doing *(hand)*
4. A shift in commitment *(habit)*

Transformation requires the courage to trust the process. Many claim they want to grow, but very few want to experience the growing pains that come with the transformation process. To fully open yourself to the transformation process, you have to have the courage to do what must be done even when it is difficult, uncomfortable, inconvenient, or risky. Most bail during the transformation phase because they lack the courage to become uncomfortable during difficult moments of change. To help people through the painful stages of change that include shifts in the "heart, head, hands, and habits," I recommend a behavioral change process known in the field of public health as "the stages of change." These include: (1) pre-contemplation; (2) contemplation; (3) preparation; (4) action; and (5) maintenance. I have adapted them below to apply to changes necessary for achieving one's full potential.

Stage 1: Pre-contemplation. The first step in the transformation process is called the pre-contemplation stage. At this stage, most people are not really thinking about taking action. This stage of transformation is really preserved for lifting the fog towards beginning to think clearly and gain clarity on the changes you must make to live the life you dream about. Most people who are open to life coaching typically have already transcended the pitfalls associated with the pre-contemplation phase. However, for the purposes of this book, I want to identify the characteristics and behaviors of individuals in the pre-contemplation stage to help you guard against returning to this phase.

People in the pre-contemplation phase are unable or unwilling to take full responsibility for their own problematic behavior. Some individuals at this phase may experience an initial burst of zeal or inspiration, but they tend to undervalue the pros of changing and are inclined to overestimate the cons. In doing so, they justify the lack of potential positive outcomes as a reason to avoid making major plans to change. If you ever gain the trust of someone with a lot of potential, yet discover they remain in the pre-contemplation phase for long periods of time, they are more than likely experiencing demoralization and hopelessness. They are afraid to think about changing because life from their perspective has been one painful disappointment after another. As a coping mechanism, they make peace with their inner under-achieving self.

Stage 2: Contemplation. When I sold Mary Kay, my director had a favorite quote, "What we think about, we bring about." This is the essence of the contemplation phase of transformation. The contemplation phase is where you begin focusing on: (1) what you really want (purpose); (2) how bad you want it (passion); and (3) why you want it (motivation).

The contemplation phase centers on thinking about how you will go about getting what your heart desires. The work that needs to be done is to align your heart with your mind. There is a time element that needs to be considered in the contemplation phase so as to avoid shocking your current system, thereby causing it to shut down. First, make an "undo" or "not-to do" list. Then for the first 30 days, set goals that "undo" bad habits and personally inflicted mal-practices. Then set goals that you want to achieve in the next 90 days. Identify 3-5 goals that constitute "quick wins" that typically consist of projects you have neglected, or goals you have abandoned in the past. The 3-5 goals on this list ideally are meant to demonstrate that you are capable of lighting your own fire and finishing what you started. Finally, identify goals 6-10 goals that you can see yourself achieving in the next six (6) months. For all these goals at the 30- day, 90-day and 6-month mark, develop a baseline assessment that tells you where you are starting from. Then select dates on the calendar that mark the end-goal date and the goal that is to be attained. Then journal as to why it is so important to you that you achieve this goal now and within this time period. Pinpoint why you have procrastinated and highlight what you are going to do differently this time to achieve it. Journal about how achieving these goals will make a difference in your life.

Many people remain in the contemplation stage for years because they have so many factors and barriers that keep them from preparing to take action. Write down every barrier and challenge you can think of that will keep you from achieving each goal identified at the 30-day, 90-day and 6-month intervals. Then identify the actions you are willing to take to eliminate each barrier.

Stage 3: Preparation. In the preparation stage, you want to experiment with small changes in preparation for taking action. During this phase, it is important to develop a firm, detailed scheme for actions that you will complete at the 30-, 90-day, and 6-month time intervals. In fact, your action plans should consist of a "not to do list" as this list is just as significant as your "to do list."

View the first 30 days as a detoxing and detachment process for the most part. Become more conscious of your plan to undo bad habits, mal-practices, and identify critical tasks that must be done to give you a morale boost. This will put you in a better position to take action as discussed in the next phase. However, in this phase, you are beginning to properly align the head, heart, and hands to work towards a transformed life. In order for your 30-day preparation and planning phase to be effective, a key task that must be completed during this phase revolves around that of preparing close family, friends, and business associates that you are about to take

119

action for the next level of achievement in your life. You should also be aligning yourself with likeminded individuals who are on a similar quest for achievement. If you do not include these people in realignment activities in your preparation stage, then you lower your chances for achieving your change goals.

Stage 4: Take Action. This stage of taking action is the equivalent of starting where you are towards achieving the 30-day, 90-day, and 6-month goals you set. Bring forth the planning tasks completed in stages two (2) and three (3) and commit to doing the work. In taking action you must distinguish between activity and productivity. Assess consistently whether or not the actions you are taking are moving you closer to your goal or simply keeping you busy. The action phase is where you are tested and tempted to seek refuge from the pain and strain associated with transformation. This is when you need to recall your fortitude plan and resolve to persevere as it is the glue that holds the work done in stages two (2), three (3), and four (4) together under pressure.

Stage 5: Maintenance. You arrive at the fifth stage of maintenance when you have completed your six (6) month goals. In essence, what is your game plan for not retreating to a "corner of comfort"? Now you must institutionalize the necessary habits to avoid relapsing to old behaviors of mediocrity. When you hear the word "relapse" you should be thinking in the humble sense of that of an addicted personality that has made incredible strides to change harmful activities into something more productive only to fall back on destructive behavior. Because of the significance of a solid maintenance plan, the entire next chapter on motivation centers on how to build and adhere to a robust plan to remain motivated to keep striving beyond the 6-month goal attainment. For this chapter on transformation, I present nine (9) of the 40 achievement principles designed as guidance for changing your life into the one you dream about.

PRINCIPLES FOR TRANSFORMATION

T	THINK AND MOVE	
R	RISKS	
A	ADDICTIONS	
N	NEUTRALIZE NAYSAYERS	
S	SUCCESS FRAMEWORK	
F	FAIL FORWARD	
O	OPTIONS AND OPPORTUNITIES	
R	RADICAL RESULTS	
M	MIRROR MOMENTS	

Let's Go to Work!

Transformation: Suggested Playlist

Song *(Artist)*

1. Black Butterfly *(Denise Williams)*

2. Black Butterfly *(Sounds of Blackness)*

3. Man in the Mirror *(Michael Jackson)*

4. Feeling Good *(Nina Simone) (Jennifer Hudson)*

5. Control *(Janet Jackson)*

6. Everything Must Change *(Nina Simone) (George Benson) (Oleta Adams)*

7. A Change is Gonna Come *(Sam Cooke)*

8. A Brand New Kind of Me *(Alicia Keys)*

9. I Know I've Been Changed *(LaShun Pace)*

10. Clean Inside *(Hezekiah Walker)*

11. Wake Up Everybody *(Harold Melvin & The Blue Notes)*

12. Pieces of Me *(Ledisi)*

13. Conquer *(Estelle)*

14. The Potter's House *(Tramaine Hawkins)*

15. Still I Rise *(Yolanda Adams)*

16. I'll Take You There *(The Staple Singers)*

17. Move on Up *(Curtis Mayfield)*

18. Higher Ground *(Stevie Wonder)*

19. A Whole New World *(Aladdin)*

20. Circle of Life *(Lion King)*

Think and Move

"Only in the process of moving forward do your creative thoughts gain enough strength to ultimately become a thing."

Dr. Quinn Motivates

Once clear that change must happen, creative individuals and high achievers invest in learning how to "think and move." In working with creative thinkers over the years I have discovered that they have a very difficult time deciding when the timing is right to move on a creative idea that they have been nurturing for a long period of time. The concept of thinking and moving assumes that you are committed to pursue higher aspirations, have clarity on what you are pursuing, and are now ready to invest in the action necessary to achieve greater goals. The key is that you are now in motion to transform "thoughts to things."

The primary reason individuals avoid moving forward on innovative ideas is most desire perfect conditions prior to being thrust into the public. On some levels this may be appropriate because the public is filled with dream killers, who if it is not a perfect creation, will rip it apart. But there are some planning activities that one can employ to coincide with the creative thinking process that demonstrate one is very intentional about making progress toward the completion line.

As you are thinking and moving, be prepared to address a plethora of unprecedented issues. Things that you have never encountered or confronted will come seemingly out of the air and obscure your view of the road ahead. When they do, you must be quick to problem solve before a spirit of procrastination sets in and derails your uptick in movement. When faced with seemingly insurmountable obstacles, ask yourself, "What's the worst that could happen?" If the answer is that no one will be harmed, and perhaps someone's ego might get bruised, then keep it moving. Apply problem solving skills using the "F" method: (1) frame the issue; (2) find the facts; (3) facilitate feedback; (4) focus on what is feasible; (5) finalize a plan of action; then (6) forward move!

It's time to go to Work: "Think and Move"

"No problem can be solved by the same consciousness that created it. We need to see the world anew."

Albert Einstein

One of the best tools for learning to think and move on multiple dimensions is American author, speaker, and Pastor John Maxwell's work on "How Successful People Think" where he identifies 11 thinking paradigms used by high-achieving individuals. Among the 11 dimensions of thinking like a successful person, there are six (6) in the table below that are essential in the early phase of transforming into an individual determined to achieve extraordinary goals.

JOHN MAXWELL'S DIMENSIONS OF HOW SUCCESSFUL PEOPLE THINK	
DIVERSE DIMENSIONS OF "THINKING"	**SUGGESTED "MOVEMENT" TO ENHANCE YOUR THINKING**
CULTIVATE BIG-PICTURE THINKING	• Engage in continuous learning from diverse sources and in diverse settings • Establish a vision of what success looks like • Resist the need to be exact or certain at this level of thinking • Explore unchartered territories and unorthodox strategies
ENGAGE IN FOCUSED THINKING	• Gain clarity on a course of action • Remove distractions by identifying what you need to give up to go up • Make time to focus in solitude • Set goals and chart your progress
HARNESS CREATIVE THINKING	• Explore options without restraints and limits • Embrace ambiguity and illogical • Ignore creativity killers • Interact with creative geniuses • Participate in activities outside of your comfort zone
EMPLOY REALISTIC THINKING	• Fact find • Weigh pros and cons including identifying the worst and best case scenario • Identify resources
UTILIZE STRATEGIC THINKING	• Compartmentalize issues into manageable parts • Form a compelling "WHY" you will move in a particular directions • Assess your resources • Develop detail plans and processes
RELY ON BOTTOM-LINE THINKING	• Answer the question: "What's the end game"? • Set measures and markers to chart progress towards goal completion

Risks

You cannot transform from where you are to a life of fulfilled goals and aspirations without taking risks. Risk-taking is not the same as being reckless. Risk-taking in this context centers on taking actions to achieve your dreams in a way that increases your chances of failure. Risk-taking is really about opening yourself to change and being courageous enough to communicate those changes to everyone who has become comfortable with your current state of being. It is accepting full responsibility for assuring that all systems are go in moving your life to where you imagine it should be.

In preparing for risk-taking weigh the pros and cons. If your pros outweigh your cons, then develop a game plan for addressing multiple variables aimed at achieving a positive result. Interestingly enough, when it comes to risk-taking, the planning and take-action formula is similar to that of losing weight. If you eat less high-calorie food and exercise more, then over time you get the positive result of weight loss. But the intervening variables force this simple formula into a more complicated model. In like manner, risk-taking is setting goals and removing obstacles that hinder achieving them. However, many factors serve as barriers to activating this simple risk-taking formula.

The real work is in developing a risk-management plan to enhance your motivation for taking on calculated risks. In addition, you must eliminate those areas of your life that serve as barriers to risk taking. There are at least four types of hindrances to risk-taking: (1) self-imposed; (2) socially-constructed; (3) systemic; and (4) structural.

It's time to go to Work: "Risk"

"If you don't take risks, you'll have a wasted soul."
Drew Barrymore

In my work, I have identified the most common reasons people avoid taking risks. Assess your reasons for being risk averse within the context of whether or not it is: (1) self-imposed by you; (2) socially-constructed based on your interaction with others; (3) systemically tied to your connection to family, educational, religious, economic, or political values; or (4) structural, meaning built into the historical inequities of society.

DR. QUINN'S SELF-ASSESSSMENT OF BARRIERS TO RISK-TAKING				
HINDRANCES TO RISK-TAKING	SELF-IMPOSED	SOCIALLY-CONSTRUCTED	SYSTEMIC	STRUCTURAL
1. Fear of rejection				
2. Need for approval				
3. Need to know <u>all</u> the "ins and outs" of a situation before committing				
4. Desire to avoid conflict				
5. Lack of belief in yourself and others				
6. Intellectualizing to avoid action				
7. Fear of being labeled incompetent				
8. Fear of failure				
9. Fear of success				
10. Pain avoidance				
11. A need for security				
12. Inability to let go of an old belief				
13. Substance use/abuse "clouding" your thinking				
14. Fear of hurting others				
15. Fear of losing the love of significant others				
16. Unwillingness to accept possible negative consequences				
17. Poor role modeling in family of origin				
18. Confusion about requirements to change				
19. Overly comfortable in playing life safe				
20. Rationalizing that someone else needs to take action first				

Notes to Self on "Risk"

ADDICTIONS

"Until you name and address the pain, you will always find a way to justify overindulging in even the good things in life that become an addiction."

Dr. Quinn Motivates

In our society we have been socialized to minimize pain and maximize pleasure. Over time pain management can evolve into an addiction. What's even more pronounced is how we conveniently separate "good" and "bad" addictions. In fact, we have constructed a vibrant recovery community around socially unacceptable addictions such as alcohol, eating, gambling, hoarding, illicit drugs, sexual or even shopping. Because of the complicated nature of diagnosing and treating addictions, I am limited to a thesis of raising awareness that addictions include any behaviors used as a substitute to minimize pain over longer periods of time.

In an attempt to minimize pain and maximize pleasure, a number of socially-acceptable behaviors can become addictions. These addictions that are socially acceptable may include, but are not limited to: (1) shopping, (2) technology, (3) social media, (4) romance, (5) engaging in multiple relationships, (6) power tripping and controlling, (7) religiosity, (8) community service, (9) working, (10) partying, (11) pathological lying, (12) overprotecting one's own children, (13) underachieving, and (14) overachieving, just to name a few that you would not normally label as "addictive behaviors."

There is another category of pain numbing behaviors known as "maladaptive behaviors" where individuals display dysfunctional inter-personal responses to otherwise "normal' interactions. These pain numbing behaviors include: (1) defensive or rigid reactions, (2) denial and blaming, (3) aloofness and avoidance, and (4) detachment and uncaring. Whether labeled as good or bad, a substance or activity, the methodology for addressing self–defeating behaviors that have become addictive entails the same humbling steps as described in the work section that follows.

IT'S TIME TO GO TO WORK: "ADDICTION"

"When you abuse drugs or alcohol or any of its socially-accepted substitutes, you are not getting high, you are getting temporary relief from the lows in your life."
Patrick Kennedy

The recovery process for self-defeating behaviors that limit higher aspirations is the same as the humbling steps to address "bad addictions," such as addiction to drugs and alcohol, sex, gambling, and food just to name a few. Many can rely upon non-clinical strategies to address the causes and consequences associated with minimizing pain. However, do not be ashamed should you need clinical care or legally prescribed and professionally managed medication to address chemical imbalances in the brain that cause mood swings and disorders, and perhaps lead to addictions as coping strategies.

THE 12 STEPS TO RECOVERY FROM "NORMAL ADDICTIONS"
(same as the traditional 12 steps to recovery)

STEP 1	• Admit that you are powerless over self-defeating behavior that you are using to numb or avoid pain.
STEP 2	• Intensify your relationship with God.
STEP 3	• Make a decision to become fully dependent upon God for care and comfort.
STEP 4	• Identify moral and character flaws that are causes and consequences of your compulsive lifestyle.
STEP 5	• Be transparent about the hurt, harm, and danger you have caused others.
STEP 6	• Be entirely ready to have God remove character flaws you identified in step four.
STEP 7	• Humbly ask God to remove your shortcomings.
STEP 8	• Put a name on and nature of the harm you caused others.
STEP 9	• Make attempts to make amends for the wrong you caused others, unless you perceive that to do so will injure that person further.
STEP 10	• Continue to engage in self-awareness and make changes as you discover behaviors that are detrimental to yourself and others.
STEP 11	• Commit to a life of prayer and meditation to guard against relapse.
STEP 12	• Share your story.

Neutralize Naysayers

"When you own your own story, you automatically neutralize negativity."
Dr. Quinn Motivates

If you really knew how much negativity permeates into your sub-conscious after years of conditioning, it would literally blow your mind. As a matter of fact, negativity in our society has become so normalized that we wear the status of being in the middle of the pack as a badge of honor. Economically, we strive for middle-class status. In school we strive for a solid B average. In corporate America, mid-level manager becomes the coveted career aspiration. If being in the middle is truly where your potential and comfort level lies, then by all means live a decent, comfortable middle-class life style. But if your heart and soul longs for greater aspirations, you will have to develop an ironclad strategy for neutralizing naysayers.

The trouble with naysayers is that they tend to be in your private, intimate, and social space. For most with a thick enough skin, it is effortless to ignore negative comments from people we don't know or those whose opinions we don't value. Dr. Martin Luther King's "Letter from a Birmingham Jail" is a prime example, as embedded in his letter is a degree of hurt that he has to address the negativity from inside his own base about his strategy to achieve civil rights. However, if you continue to read it, not only does he neutralize the naysayers, but he restates the bigger picture, reiterates the strategy, and reminds the reader of who the real enemy is.

When it comes to naysayers, it is important to remember that not every negative statement requires a response. Don't turn an ignorant statement into an unproductive conversation. You make naysayers relevant when you give them valuable time in attempting to win them over. In essence, resist the need to defend and explain your decisions to pursue greatness.

IT'S TIME TO GO TO WORK: "NEUTRALIZE NAYSAYERS"

"Remembering that I'll be dead soon is the most important tool I've ever encountered to help me make the big choices in life. Because almost everything - all external expectations, all pride, all fear of embarrassment or failure - these things just fall away in the face of death, leaving only what is truly important."

Steve Jobs

The problem with addressing naysayers is that you never know when and how they are going to strike. Some are passive and present with "concerns" or "disappointments," while others are more active-aggressive, and perhaps even confrontational. In either extreme, the bottom line is naysayers can potentially use up a lot of your time and energy needed to advance your goals. Use the following ten (10) points as guidance to neutralizing naysayers, and thereby avoid non-productive exchanges with irrelevant individuals.

DR. QUINN'S GUIDANCE TO GUARD AGAINST UNHEALTHY NAYSAYERS

1. Determine the difference between haters who are just "popping off at the mouth" and enemies who are putting in work to damage your reputation and sabotage your success. Haters can be ignored, but enemies must be dealt with.
2. Increase your capacity to live a vulnerable and transparent life, which is the best offense against anything a naysayer may vocalize.
3. Don't alter your achievement strategy to win the admiration of non-essential naysayers.
4. If the naysayer in question is a valuable and contributing member to your life, then invest "some" time in understanding their "concerns" related to your pursuit of higher achievement.
5. Determine your "rise above it" strategy to negativity that is brought directly to you from a third party telling you what "others" are saying.
6. If you choose to respond to naysayers, do so in a non-personal, non-threatening, and definitive manner where you address the main issue and commit to move on.
7. Resist being baited into a social media war in response to naysayers.
8. Guard your progress and process towards achieving your goal.
9. Recognize the power of emotions when hearing negativity about you.
10. Draw inspiration for responding to naysayers from Dr. King's "Letter from a Birmingham Jail.

Success Framework

"Success is bringing your full self to a structured process of becoming significant."
Dr. Quinn Motivates

One of the most recurring questions young professional women I mentor and/or manage have is, "What do I need to do to become successful?" In answering this question over the last 20 years, I have developed what I call the "Success Framework" comprised of core elements that should be incorporated into a customized success plan. This framework only applies to individuals who have already done the hard work of identifying overall professional goals and objectives. Then you are ready to apply the core elements of the "Success Framework" as a model for achieving those goals. The core definitions of the ten (10) components comprising the framework continue on the work page portion.

1. **SUBSTANCE.** There is no substitute for substance. You must work intensely to become a subject matter expert no matter your chosen profession.

2. **STYLE.** Style represents one's total package. It includes one's personal styling (wardrobe, hair, and make-up). In addition, style refers to how you fully present in public, including body language, mannerism, speech, tone, perceived attitude, and level of engagement with others.

3. **SAVVY.** Savvy typically refers to one's ability to present as personable, professional, and politically balanced within one's operating environment. It includes one's ability to integrate: (1) knowledge (learned substance and intelligence); (2) wisdom (experience and historical knowledge); and (3) discernment (gut, hunch, insight, intuition, perception) when making strategic decisions and interacting with key stakeholders.

4. **STANDARDS.** Standards are defined as bottom line measures of "excellence". Setting standards of excellence is a combination of what is the norm for high performance in the field or industry within which you operate and one's personally established markers of quality.

"Success is to be measured not so much by the position that one has reached in life as by the obstacles which he has overcome."

Booker T. Washington

5. **STRATEGY.** Strategy refers to one's game plan. Your game plan must reflect you as a solo player, and as a team player. In either case, you must study the competition, work with the coach, practice, and play your position in a way that leads to being a franchise player.

6. **SPIRITUALITY.** Spirituality refers to the need to rely upon some faith-centered belief system as a moral compass. Spirituality is about how your behavior will be driven by character and integrity.

7. **SELF-DISCIPLINE.** Self-discipline speaks to the degree to which you are willing to adhere to a strict regimen of rules, regulations, and protocols as imposed by organizations and governments. Other portions of self-discipline are derived from personal sacrifices and struggles utilized to get the results as outlined in one's overall success schema.

8. **SELF-AWARENESS.** Self-awareness is an intense process of exploring multiple dimensions of ones' self. For more, refer to the comprehensive perspective on self-awareness as outlined in the chapter on "inspiration" where I identify 40 dimensions of "self" compartmentalized into four (4) domains, including: (1) good self; (2) social construction of self; (3) bad self; and (4) open to changing oneself.

9. **SYNERGY.** Synergy centers on a spirit of cooperation. Synergizing is about one's ability to work well with others based on a mutuality of purpose, shared values, and the degree to which there is chemistry between individuals who have to work together.

10. **SIGNIFICANCE.** Significance is about what difference your life makes in the lives of others. What do you want your legacy to be? Why and how will your life matter beyond your lifetime?

Fail Forward

"In life if you are going to achieve anything great you have to be willing to fail better."
Dr. Quinn Motivates

If you are ever going to achieve anything great, you will have to make friends with failure. Failure is that friend that will show up at the most inopportune time imaginable along the journey of transformation. If you are not afraid of failure, then you have a lot more strategies at your disposal for achieving your greatest aspiration. The problem with failure is that all the key socializing agencies in our society train us to fear failure, and thus anticipate being humiliated, punished, or sidelined if we fail. I reject this narrative of a culture of fear of failure by immersing myself in a study of how creative thinkers and high achievers face failures and setbacks. What I discovered is that these individuals view failure totally different from the rest of the world. What would kill the spirits and efforts of a normal person serves as fuel and enthusiasm to get up and try something different for the high achiever. Here is a list of common themes among creative thinkers and high achievers in the aftermath of failure:

1. They accept failure as a normal part of the path to success.
2. They never lost self-confidence in their ability to reach a goal.
3. They remained grounded in a strong sense of purpose.
4. They didn't make excuses or blame others for having failed.
5. They took great measures to perfect variables that contributed to failure.
6. They were not afraid to reinvent themselves.
7. They work extremely hard to recover, regroup, recommit, and rebound.
8. They have a thick skin in accepting unfair hits and criticism.
9. They knew when to defend and when to keep it moving.
10. They were not afraid to be even more radical or aggressive in the turn-around strategy.

It's Time to Go to Work: "Fail Forward"

"For every failure, there's an alternative course of action. You just have to find it. When you come to a roadblock, take a detour."

Mary Kay Ash

Apply my "12-Step Formula for Making Friends with Failure" as a way to fail better and fail forward.

DR. QUINN'S 12-STEP FORMULA FOR MAKING FRIENDS WITH FAILURE		
STEP 1	FEEL IT	• Build a tolerance for experiencing a full range of emotions after a major setback while resisting the need to attack, blame, or medicate the pain.
STEP 2	FOCUS	• Focus on your strengths, talents, skills, and resources.
STEP 3	FELLOWSHIP	• Remain committed to a personal relationship with God through prayer, meditation, and biblical study, fellowshipping, and serving in ministry.
STEP 4	FACE FEARS	• Accept fear as a constant companion.
STEP 5	FORGIVE	• Forgive yourself and others for negative thoughts, words, or actions that may have been exchanged.
STEP 6	FREE YOURSELF	• Remove all buts, barriers, boundaries and barricades.
STEP 7	FIRE-UP	• You have to resolve to bounce back.
STEP 8	FIGHT	• Fight for what you believe is your life's purpose.
STEP 9	FACE IT AND FIX IT	• When you resolve to fight, you need to spend some time fixing what went wrong.
STEP 10	FINISH	• Finish what you started or what you failed at even if it's late.
STEP 11	FORWARD	• Don't allow failure to stand in the way of you taking new risks.
STEP 12	FAIL BETTER	• Immerse yourself in the stories of famous people who failed better.

Notes to Self on "Fail Forward"

OPTIONS AND OPPORTUNITIES

"You cannot fully explore options and take advantage of opportunities if you are bogged down in addressing recurring obstacles."

Dr. Quinn Motivates

Once you begin the transformation process towards higher aspirations, remain open to explore alternative options and opportunities that may not have been part of the initial strategic plan. When you think about options and opportunities, it is important to remember that they tend to have no slow or down time, and when they come your way, you have to be willing to take advantage and go. Exercising options and opportunities does not make you flighty and non-committal. It makes you shrewd, flexible, and competitive in your pursuit of goals. The shallowness sets in with options and opportunities when you know you have something great and it is working, yet you prematurely abandon the process without fully vetting the alternative. Options and opportunities should be fully explored on multiple dimensions when assessing one's operating environments and resources. Options and opportunities should be vetted against ones' bottom line, deal breakers, values, and standards of excellence.

The value of options and opportunities is that you tend to be optimistic when it comes to the future. Having options and opportunities allow you to not be victimized by setbacks or losses. We embrace challenges with confidence and vitality. Options and opportunities allow you to present as flexible in that you are open to the opinions of others during times of crises, challenges and strategic planning. Options and opportunities are most valuable when variables and key assumptions upon which you based your initial plan do not pan out. Options represent your contingency plan or worse-case scenario analysis. Keeping options open is a constant reminder that you have the power and freedom to make a different choice.

It's Time to Go to Work: "Options and Opportunities"

"Opportunities are usually disguised as hard work, so most people don't recognize them."
Ann Landers

When working with individuals wishing to explore options and opportunities I use motivational speaker Patricia Russell-McCloud's themes in her book titled "A is for Attitude" as a brainstorming tool. I love the words she uses because they lend themselves to being open to multiple levels of thinking about achievement. My key take-away when reading her book is that options and opportunities tend to flow more readily to those who have a great attitude, are assertive about their desire to achieve more, and are aggressive in pursuit of options and opportunities that get you closer to your aspirations.

PATRICIA RUSSELL-MCCLOUD'S PERSPECTIVE ON MAXIMIZING OPTIONS AND OPPORTUNITIES			
A	Attitude	**N**	Now
B	Brain power	**O**	Organization
C	Courage	**P**	Preparation
D	Dedication	**Q**	Questions
E	Effort	**R**	Risk
F	Freedom	**S**	Survival
G	Genius	**T**	Truth
H	Heritage	**U**	Unity
I	Intuition	**V**	Vision
J	Justice	**W**	Willpower
K	Know-How	**X**	X-ray
L	Life	**Y**	You
M	Meditation	**Z**	Zodiac

NOTES TO SELF ON "OPTIONS AND OPPORTUNITIES"

RADICAL RESULTS

"Radical results require rigorous work and unprecedented sacrifice and investments."

Dr. Quinn Motivates

Transforming to the next level of creative genius and high achieving will require some radical actions if you intend to produce some radial results. My model for achieving radical results transcends the "SMART goals" model. Although there are various deviations, most sources spell out the acronym for "SMART" as Specific, Measureable, Achievable, Results-focused, and Time-bound. My model centers on the more active aspects of the SMART goals model, and takes an acronym I call "ACHIEVE". "ACHIEVE" is a reminder that "SMART" goals only get achieved when we do the work to obtain the results.

DR. QUINN'S "ACHIEVE" MODEL FOR RADICAL RESULTS
A • **AFFIRM YOUR ASPIRATIONS.** Tell the truth about what you really want to achieve in this life time.
C • **CONFIRM YOUR COMMITMENT.** Develop a compelling WHY you want to achieve the goals listed as part of affirming your aspirations.
H • **HARMONIZE YOUR HEAD, HEART, HANDS, AND HABITS.** Highlight how you plan to make it happen. Devise a well-coordinated action plan for connecting your head, heart, hands, and habits.
I • **IGNITE INNOVATIVE IDEAS.** Recognize the need for creativity and innovation in achieving your goal. Resist the need to be logical, or accurate. Let your imagination run wild. Take an "anything" is possible mentality towards achieving that to which you aspire.
E • **ELIMINATE EXCUSES.** Address all "buts," "barriers," "boundaries," and "barricades" blocking your ability to achieve your greatest aspiration.
V • **VISUALIZE VICTORY.** Paint a picture of what victory looks like using the vision board process.
E • **EXECUTE WITH EXCELLENCE.** Accept that goals worth achieving require work. Avoid short cuts, excuses, and hook ups. Instead, be fully responsible for every action item associated with your goals.

IT'S TIME TO GO TO WORK: "RADICAL RESULTS"

"True stability results when presumed order and presumed disorder are balanced. A truly stable system expects the unexpected, is prepared to be disrupted, and waits to be transformed."

Tom Robbins

My "ACHIEVE" model aimed at higher aspirations works best when it is matched with principles of characters, values, morals, and integrity. I suggest using W. Clement Stones' core principles for achievement as organized into 17 principles by author Samuel Cypert.

W. CLEMENT STONES' 17 PRINCIPLES FOR ACHIEVEMENT	
ATTITUDINAL PRINCIPLES	1. A Positive Mental Attitude
	2. Definiteness of Purpose
	3. Going the Extra Mile
	4. Learning from Defeat
PERSONAL PRINCIPLES	5. Personal Initiative
	6. Enthusiasm
	7. A Pleasing Personality
	8. Self-discipline
	9. Budgeting Time and Money
	10. Maintaining Sound Physical and Mental health
FRATERNAL PRINCIPLES	11. The Master-mind Alliance
	12. Teamwork
INTELLECTUAL PRINCIPLES	13. Creative Vision
	14. Controlled Attention
	15. Accurate Thinking
SPIRITUAL PRINCIPLES	16. Applied Faith
	17. Using the Cosmic Habit Force

Mirror Moment

"Every mirror moment has within it the power to liberate or lock up the mind depending upon what you see."

Dr. Quinn Motivates

Everyone has had a mirror moment when you simply did not like the image staring back at you. We have all watched celebrities take bold and public steps to address weight and image issues. None is more memorable than the way in which Oprah Winfrey has battled with weight over the course of her creative and high-achieving strides. We even watched one woman who built a comedy career on publically calling skinny women "evil" quietly exit the stage and embark upon a radical weight loss strategy. The truth is our society has us overwhelmed and overly consumed with physical beauty. We spend billions annually to cover flaws, cut fat in half, and erase any signs of aging. Clearly, high-achieving individuals are not protected from the "mirror moment" where many justify not pushing forward with our goals and dreams because we are terrified of the potential body shaming that awaits us should we enter the public as anything less than flawless. Reality is we get one body and we are responsible for caring for it and protecting it. My methodology for doing so, however begins from the inside out using a formula I call "IMAGE", where I am very clear that if we are made in the image of the Divine then we are indeed wondrous. It is what happens to us along the growth process that damages and distorts our view of ourselves as "perfect the way we are."

DR. QUINN'S "IMAGE" ASSESSMENT FRAMEWORK		
I	IDENTITY	• Who am I from the inside out? (A look into the soul)
M	MIRROR	• What do I see when I look at me? (Facing the flaws)
A	AGE	• Am I aging gracefully or showing signs of worrying and weariness?
G	GENETICS	• How happy am I with that which I have inherited from my ancestors?
E	EATING AND EXERCISING	• Am I taking good care of the physical body that houses my soul?

IT'S TIME TO GO TO WORK: "MIRROR MOMENT"

"Here's an exercise to help you find inner resources: Stand in front of a mirror and look as deeply as you can into your eyes for 90 seconds. Don't blink, don't move your eyes, blur out everything else in the mirror, and block out all of the noises you hear. Focus only your eyes. This exercise will teach you how to reach into your soul and find that inner strength that will allow you to continue your march forward even when things seem to be getting tough. What you're looking at in the mirror is your essence, your drive your determination to make a big change in your life."
Dr. Ian K. Smith

"What I know for sure is that the struggle is over. I've finally made peace with my body."
Oprah Winfrey

"Before you embark upon a weight-loss program, spend some time exploring what's really weighing you down."
Dr. Quinn Motivates

Unfortunately, many are holding themselves hostage towards pursuing greater goals because they don't like what looks back at them during "mirror moments." Let's face it. When it comes to the physical body, you have three options. You can: (1) be ashamed, (2) accept it, or (3) adjust it. However, before you spend money on another weight loss regimen, answer the following questions in an effort to discover what is weighing heavy on you about your body image:

1. How was body image discussed in your home and among your peers growing up?
2. What is happening in your work and social environment today that impacts how you feel about your physical shape?
3. What emotional triggers contribute to you feeling bad about your body?
4. What does your self-care regimen consist of?
5. What do you feel like you have missed out on in life because you have avoided addressing those things that concern you about your anatomy?
6. What are you willing to change to get the body image you desire?
7. How will a changed body image change the way you approach creativity and high achievement?

Notes to Self on "Mirror Moment"

MOTIVATION

"The reason (s) one has for acting or behaving in a particular way."

"If your motives are wrong, no amount of motivation will ever be right. You will move for a minute, but you will never have the defining moment that launches you forward."

Dr. Quinn Motivates

When it comes to sustaining motivation, you must find a compelling WHY! The last phase of creativity and high achievement is to remain motivated once you have begun making significant strides towards reaching your potential. In its simplest form, the best motivation is having a compelling "WHY." When engaging individuals in goal setting, they tend to focus on their "I" story. I redirect them to their "WHY" story. The strength of the "WHY" one desires something different is a primary predictor of whether or not they will reach the goal no matter how big or small. A weak "WHY" typically is supported by excuses and explanations of why one is limited in pursuit of one's goals.

Balance the two primary forms of motivation. When it comes to reaching one's highest potential, you must strengthen your "WHY" by integrating two primary sources of motivation: (1) extrinsic and (2) intrinsic. Extrinsic motivators are those that arise from outside of the individual and often involve rewards such as trophies, money, social recognition or praise. Extrinsic motivation can also come from the threat of punishment for misbehavior. Intrinsic motivation involves responses to biological, emotional, social, and cognitive forces that activate behavior. Collectively, intrinsic and extrinsic motivators unlock barriers and unleash the beast within to pursue lifelong dreams, goals, and higher aspiration.

Put motivation into practice. Here are five (5) questions to guide you from moving extrinsic and intrinsic motivation from theory to practice.

1. *Purpose:* What am I called to do?
2. *Goals:* What am I supposed to accomplish as a direct result of my calling?

3. *Motivation:* Why do I want to accomplish these selected goals?
4. *Strategy:* How do I accomplish my goals as tied to the calling on my life?
5. *Practices:* What steps, tasks, daily activities must I undertake in order to fulfill the life purpose for which I was called?

Reconcile motives and motivation. Combining intrinsic and extrinsic motivators for optimum drive towards a goal is highly dependent upon "motives". Motives manifest as intent. If you have hidden motives then you will minimize the amount of resources and relationships that come your way to help you achieve your goal. If you are transparent and intentional about sharing your motives with a supportive team, you maximize the degree of motivation that flows through you to get it done. The beginning of intent is to have an internal conversation with yourself where you are clear on your mission and what it takes to make it happen.

In this chapter I focus on strategies for balancing extrinsic and intrinsic motivation. The key to remaining motivated is to share the enthusiasm and wisdom with others. The truth is before I penned the *40 achievement principles* I practiced them and shared them freely with anyone who would listen, which is how I got the nickname "Dr. Quinn Motivates." Each of the nine (9) principles in this section on motivation is designed to help you balance extrinsic and intrinsic motivation as enthusiasm that moves you closer to your aspirations.

PRINCIPLES FOR MOTIVATION	
M	MEMORABLE MOMENTS AND MILESTONES
O	ORDER AND ORGANIZATION
T	TIME
I	INTENTIONALITY
V	VULNERABILITY
A	AFFIRMATION
T	TIMING
E	EMPOWERED FOR LIFE

Let's Go to Work!

NOTES TO SELF ON "MOTIVATION"

MOTIVATION: SUGGESTED PLAYLIST

Song (Artist)

1. It's Time for the Motivator (Dr. Quinn Motivates)

2. Eye of the Tiger (Survivor)

3. Get Up (Mary Mary)

4. I Feel Good (James Brown)

5. Gonna Be A Lovely Day (Kirk Franklin and The Nu Nation Project)
   A Lovely Day (Bill Withers)

6. I'm Every Woman (Chaka Khan) (Whitney Houston)

7. What a Feeling (Irene Cara/Flash Dance Soundtrack)

8. Ease on Down the Road (The Wiz Soundtrack)

9. Green Light (John Legend featuring Andre 3000)

10. Cantaloop (Flip Fantasia)

11. Let's Get it Started (M.C. Hammer)

12. Push it (Salt & Pepa)

13. 99 and a Half (Hezekiah Walker & The Love Fellowship Crusade Choir)

14. Watch Me Shine (Joanna Pacitti)

15. Walking on Sunshine (Katrina & the Waves)

16. Roar (Katy Perry)

17. I'm Still Standing (Elton John)

18. I Hope you Dance (Lee Ann Womack) (Gladys Knight)

19. St. Elmo's Fire: Man In Motion (John Parr)

20. I'm a Survivor (Destiny's Child)

Memorable Moments and Milestones

"Don't miss life's memorable moments and milestones chasing five minutes of fame."
Dr. Quinn Motivates

Identify memorable moments that become defining moments. As a connoisseur of autobiographical works, I am mesmerized by the way memorable moments actually were "defining moments." What is even more impactful is how those defining moments are born out of experiences that most conceptualize as failure in our society. For those seeking to go the achievement distance, nothing is more motivational than immersing oneself in memorable moments and milestones of successful people. Of course every narrative has a "spoiler alert" because we know how the story ends. Nevertheless, reflecting on how creative and high-achieving individuals make sense of moments in time that ultimately transformed them to greatness tends to ignite a fire to fight for what you truly desire.

Memorable moments are valuable for personal insight, inspiration, and growth. In my exploration of autobiographies, a few patterns emerged in terms of how successful people find value in moments that most would label as mundane. Here are five recurring patterns I found to show how creative high achievers locate unprecedented value in memorable moments and milestones:

1. A change in attitude about setting and achieving goals previously deemed "out of reach"
2. A vulnerable and transparent examination of the meaning of failure
3. The courage to walk away from dysfunction by any means necessary
4. A willingness to re-examine old problems with a new prism of possibilities
5. A renewed commitment to complete projects that were abandoned

Pay attention to the memorable moments and milestones in your own life because these "aha moments" can be very powerful in shifting your mindset about what is possible in this life time.

It's Time to Go to Work: "Memorable Moments and Milestones"

"You have the choice this very moment- the only moment you have for certain, I hope you aren't so wrapped up in nonessential stuff that you forget to really enjoy yourself- because this moment is about to be over. I hope you'll look back and remember today as the day you decided to make every one count, to relish each hour as if there would never be another. And when you get the choice to sit out or dance, I hope you dance."

Oprah Winfrey

To help you gain a perspective on how to use memorable moments and milestones as a form of motivation, I have selected autobiographies that I believe explore the good, the bad, and the ugly of these successful people's lives. These individuals have been very transparent about personal failures and how they had to rebuild after trials and tribulations derailed their best laid plans. Dr. Maya Angelou's life was so rich with lessons learned that she wrote her autobiography in seven (7) different volumes.

Recommended reading(s):

- *What I Know for Sure by Oprah Winfrey (2014)*
- *Maya Angelou*
    - o *I Know Why the Caged Bird Sings (1969)*
    - o *Gather Together in My Name (1974)*
    - o *Singin' and Swingin' and Gettin' Merry Like Christmas (1976)*
    - o *The Heart of a Woman (1981)*
    - o *All God's Children Need Traveling Shoes (1986)*
    - o *A Song Flung Up to Heaven (2002)*
    - o *Mom & Me & Mom (2013)*
- *The Autobiography of Malcolm X as told to Alex Haley (1987)*
- *The Autobiography of Dr. Martin Luther King by Clayborne Carson (2001)*
- *The Autobiography of Andrew Carnegie (2011)*
- *Up From Slavery: The Autobiography of Booker T. Washington (1900)*
- *The Autobiography of Mary Kay (1994)*
- *Dreams from my Father: The Autobiography of Barack Obama (1995)*
- *Steve Jobs by Walter Isaacson (2011)*
- *Long Walk To Freedom: The Autobiography of Nelson Mandela (1995)*

Notes to Self on "Memorable Moments and Milestones"

ORDER AND ORGANIZATION

"Creative thinkers appear to the untrained observer as scatter brained. But don't let the random thoughts and awkward actions fool you. There is a method to the madness."

Dr. Quinn Motivate

Order and organization are necessary. In the absolute, creative thinkers and high achievers tend to have a greater tolerance for chaos and clutter on multiple levels. They have been known to create extraordinary things operating out of the most disorganized home and workspaces imaginable. This group is especially gifted with the ability to get past calamity and visualize calm. No matter how creative or high achieving you are, however, you must commit to periods of time where you focus on bringing order and organization to your world.

Remember that planning and organizing are not the enemies of creativity. In fact, as you move the clutter and chaos out of your life, you create appropriate space for your deepest perceptions to take physical shape and form. The key areas that need order and organization using a system that works for you include: (1) time management; (2) household management; (3) home office organization; (4) business administration and operations; and (5) personal finance and accounting.

Bring order to "the cluttered mind" and "the conflicted soul." This is to assure that you keep a clean and clear conscience as it could impact your character and integrity. In essence, you have to intentionally let "stuff" go in the spiritual, mental, and physical realms that could create toxic blocks. Release yourself from people, habits, and environments that no longer serve good and healthy purposes in your life. Bring order and closure by cleaning up your mistakes and give yourself permission to engage in a fresh start. Resist the need to be co-dependent with others who function under dysfunctional clutter and chaos that dumps into your life. Your perspective on order and organization is simply your gift to you. Do whatever is necessary to constantly remind yourself that you deserve a life of peace and harmony defined by you for you.

IT'S TIME TO GO TO WORK: "ORDER AND ORGANIZATION"

"In the midst of movement and chaos, keep stillness inside of you."

Deepak Chopra

In an effort to bring order and organization into your creative and innovative fold, consider a quarterly "time out" comprised of a three (3)day period to go inside yourself and environment where you re-set systems and settings governing your life. Bring order and organization to your life on multiple levels: (1) things; (2) thoughts; (3) tasks; (4) time; and (5) teams. If you run a business, set aside time to bring order and organization to the administrative and operations components for your venture. If you lack a current method for order and organization, start by using the themes below to customize your order and organization plan of action. Make it fit your personality and preferences as a way to increase the likelihood that you will maintain the systems used for order and organization.

1. **Time.** Time management entails allotting finite time to interact with others via e-mail, phone, social media, and meetings. Also, schedule what I call "executive sessions with self" where you intentionally set aside time for creating, exploring, learning, meditating, planning, playing, and worshiping.

2. **Household.** Commit to a radical household re-organization at least twice per year where you unpack and discard "stuff" that has accumulated in your closets, drawers, and spare rooms. Make an annual list of home improvements and set dates for completion. Donate gently used items to charity.

3. **Home office organization.** Decorate your home office with motivational and inspirational quotes. Play music to set the creative atmosphere in your work space and to calm you in your meditation space. Every six months, discard obsolete materials, file away important documents, and bring closure to "pet projects."

4. **Business and administration.** Designate one day per month that is your administrative day where all the administrative tasks that were tabled as non-urgent will get completed.

5. **Finance and accounting.** Take one day per month to review your personal and business finances. Check your credit report. Balance your check book. Examine your debts and set financial goals and strategies to achieve them.

6. **The cluttered mind.** Every month spend one day "downloading" all your thoughts, ideas, and hunches.

7. **The conflicted soul.** Work with intentionality to release everything that grieves your spirit and hinders you from achieving your highest level of aspiration.

NOTES TO SELF ON "ORDER AND ORGANIZATION"

TIME

"Every awesome thought must past the test of time in order to become a thing."
Dr. Quinn Motivates

No matter your background, gifts, purpose, skills, or talents, time is the great equalizing factor among all creative thinkers and high achievers. This means that a lack of time should never be an excuse for prolonged underachievement and limited progress in goal attainment.   To put it in perspective, we all have the same 60 seconds as Oprah, the same 60 minutes as Beyoncé, the same seven (7) days per week as President Obama, and the same 12 months per year as Tyler Perry. The differentiating factor is the value being placed on this expensive capital called "time". In order to see time as the great game changer, study the different dimensions of the concept of time.

DR. QUINN'S DIMENSIONS AND DEFINITIONS OF "TIME"

1. *"Time"* refers to a point of time measured in hours, minutes and seconds.

2. *"Timing"* is about a judgment call as to whether or not this is the particular time to pursue a particular course of action. Judgment calls are made based on a combination of experience, knowledge, and wisdom working together as "intuition" to give you a gut response to the question "Is the timing right for a particular initiative"? I always say, "Timing is everything as most missed opportunities are often the result of bad timing.

3. *"Timeless"* things in life are those that are ageless in that they are not impacted by the passage of time, and may even increase in value over time.

4. *"Timelines"* are meeting finite dates, deadlines, and critical paths to bring your creative aspirations and goals to a point of completion. Timelines also measure your progress.

5. *"Time management"* is personal accountability of productivity and efficiency. Personal time management skills include: goal setting, planning, prioritizing, decision-making, delegating, and scheduling.

It's time to go to Work: "Time"

"Better three hours too soon than a minute too late."
William Shakespeare

Here are some activities to move from theory to practice in using the concept of time as a valuable resource to obtain your goals.

1. Set a stopwatch for 90 seconds and answer the following question by jotting down the first thing that comes to mind without filtering: *If I had unlimited time and resources, what would I be doing?*

2. Identify the five things that are taking up way too much time in your life. Do you have compelling reasons as to why you really could benefit from letting these things go? For those things that you really could stop spending time on, develop an action plan to minimize or limit these activities and replace them with the things listed on your "unlimited time and resources" list.

3. Stephen Covey, one of the world's foremost leadership authorities, organizational experts, and thought leaders, suggests in his book that many of us are "addicted to urgencies" and get an adrenaline rush from handling crises. We become, Covey says, dependent on urgent matters for the sake of excitement and energy. He further argues that urgency addictions provide an artificial sense of self-worth, power, control, and accomplishment. If "urgencies" are your drugs of choice, what is your plan for recovery?

4. Covey's principle on time includes a paradigm for considering what matters most when it comes to how we spend our time. The essence of this paradigm is that we must make time to live, love, learn, and leave a legacy.

5. How do you balance your time in the four broad categories: mental, physical, social, and spiritual?

6. How do you make sense of Covey's quote: "The main thing is to keep the main the main thing?" What is the main thing in your life? And once identified, how do you prioritize it to keep it the main thing on your time and task lists?

7. Explore different time management systems and select one that works for your personality and preferences, and goals pursuit.

Notes to Self on "Time"

INTENTIONALITY

"Intentionality is the deliberate process of assuring your thoughts, words, and actions remain in perfect alignment."

Dr. Quinn Motivates

Be intentional about your dreams and desires. One way to remain motivated once you begin moving in the direction of high achievement is to be intentional about all your thoughts, actions, and interactions. Be very clear about what you intend to accomplish and then communicate it ever so gently throughout all of the environments within which you operate. This is because once you are intentional about your personal mission and can articulate it with clarity, the universe accommodates you. Anything less than authentic intention creates chaos and confusion that leads to complacency and continued contentment within your current comfort zone. Intentions affect every aspect of your life. For example, strong intentions create opportunities. The beauty of opportunities is that they provide choices and options. The more opportunities you create by sharing your intentions, the more empowering your decision-making process.

Stating that you are unintentional is a form of intention. One of the hardest philosophical concepts to convey is what it means to say you have no intentions or rather that one is unintentional. Reality is when you do not make a decision, prolong processes, put off major decisions, avoid responsibility, blame others for your indecisiveness, or conditional commitment, your intention is just as pronounced as if you had actually intended to delay actions. In fact, living a life full of "unintentional" choices is a passive-aggressive approach to power and control. Avoiding commitment is a socially acceptable way to guard your heart against being disappointed by your decision.

Intentionality is even more pronounced as we make choices based on our social and objective realities. Social reality refers to the subjective ways within which we see the world. Objective reality refers to the "facts" that govern our world.

It's Time to Go to Work: "Intentionality"

"Be impeccable with your word, don't take anything personally, don't make assumptions, and always do your best."

Don Miquel Ruiz

For the activity on intentionality, I have identified four layers of realities in your life where you are constantly thinking, making decisions, influencing the decisions of others, and having decisions made by others in which you must choose to comply or rebel. I have overlaid these dimensions of your everyday reality with Ruiz's agreements that include a 5th option to the original four agreements where he suggests you can change the message you deliver to yourself and to others, which is the essence of "intentionality.

KEY LIFE DIMENSIONS WITHIN THE CONTEXT OF DON MIGUEL RUIZ'S AGREEMENTS					
	BE IMPECCABLE WITH YOUR WORK	DON'T TAKE ANYTHING PERSONAL	DON'T MAKE ASSUMPTIONS	ALWAYS DO YOUR BEST	CHANGE THE MESSAGE YOU DELIVER
1. PERSONAL LIFE CHOICES					
2. FAMILY					
3. SCHOOL/WORK					
4. SOCIAL CONTACT NETWORKS					

VULNERABILITY

"Vulnerability is allowing your soul to live out loud."

Dr. Quinn Motivates

Vulnerability is a necessary condition for optimizing achievement. A willingness to yield to vulnerability puts you in the best position to reach and sustain at peak levels of performance. Vulnerability begins with telling yourself the truth about how life experiences impact you. The best way to handle being vulnerable is to be open to a comprehensive self-awareness process. Being vulnerable is different from being fragile. Fragile people break, while vulnerable people bend. Vulnerability is not a sign of weakness. To the contrary, it implies that you have the courage to be your authentic self under all circumstances.

Stop avoiding vulnerability. The reason we avoid vulnerability is we are frightened to let people know who we really are. Part of it is we have unresolved issues that we are afraid that someone will expose our deepest secrets so we intentionally hold people at a surface level of engagement. Over time, a commitment to live vulnerably prepares you to be unafraid that your deepest or darkest secrets might be exposed. In this way, being vulnerable is like lifting a great weight off you.

The threat of exposure hinders vulnerability. For those bold enough to begin the transformational process, the number one factor that stops them dead in their tracks and sends them running for cover is the threat of actual exposure of a weakness, failure, or other negative unintended consequences. Vulnerability can lead to hurt, however it is absolutely necessary to get to a higher level of achievement. It requires a transparent resolve that you are willing to risk failing and falling hard in front of everybody. However, when you allow yourself to be completely vulnerable, what you learn and experience is priceless for your overall growth and potential.

It's Time to Go to Work: "Vulnerability"

"Vulnerability is the birthplace of innovation, creativity and change."
Brené Brown

In "The Gifts of Imperfection," Brené Brown, outlined 10 guide points to engage individuals in a process towards becoming more vulnerable. The process of becoming more vulnerable may draw criticism from others that you are too emotional or "touchy feely" as our society is socially-constructed to view vulnerable people as weak and easy prey. However, deliberate choices to be vulnerable and transparent actually are a position of strength where you shift from a mindset of worrying about what people think of you to one of firmly understanding that you are enough. Use Browns' framework to identify your action plan for cultivating vulnerability in your life.

	BRENÉ BROWN'S GUIDANCE FOR CULTIVATING VULNERABILITY	
1	CULTIVATE AUTHENTICITY	• Let go of what people think about you
2	CULTIVATE SELF-COMPASSION	• Let go of perfectionism
3	CULTIVATE A RESILIENT SPIRIT	• Let go of numbing and powerlessness
4	CULTIVATE GRATITUDE AND JOY	• Let go of scarcity
5	CULTIVATE INTUITION AND TRUSTING FAITH	• Let go of the need for certainty
6	CULTIVATE CREATIVITY	• Let go of comparison
7	CULTIVATE PLAY AND REST	• Let go of exhaustion as a status symbol and productivity as self-worth
8	CULTIVATE CALM AND STILLNESS	• Let go of anxiety as a lifestyle
9	CULTIVATE MEANINGFUL WORK	• Let go of self-doubt and "supposed to"
10	CULTIVATE LAUGHTER, SONG, AND DANCE	• Let go of being cool and "always in control"

AFFIRMATIONS

"Affirmations are your way of speaking positively to old hurtful words that wounded you in the past."

Dr. Quinn Motivates

You must replace negative self-talk with positive affirmations. The reality is in our society we speak so harshly about ourselves that we label those who speak positively as looney, arrogant, or cocky. On the contrary, affirmations bring clarity to your calling and reinforce your value system of how you achieve your purpose. If appropriate, reflect on how you learned over time to view yourself negatively and speak negativity based on your socializing agents and environments. In doing so, you just may discover how easy it is for you to be consumed with negative thoughts about yourself.

If you want to change your life, then change your language. Get in the habit of listening to your language about yourself that manifests in your head and heart even if you don't always speak it publically. For some, a change of language may include an "executive session with self." "An executive session with self" is something I define as literally developing a professional agenda and conducting a meeting with yourself about important decisions you must make alone. The ability and willingness to speak in the affirmative about yourself constitutes an item that needs to be a permanent fixture on your agenda for all executive self-sessions.

Use positive affirmations to cope with negative environments from which you cannot escape or avoid so simply. Even after you have done the hard work of speaking positively about yourself, it is not uncommon for you to still encounter negativity from people in environments where you live or work. In order to survive this group, you must pour positively into their world, lest you regress to the old negative language you worked hard to overcome.

It's Time to Go to Work: "Affirmations"

"Affirmation without discipline is the beginning of delusion."
Jim Rohn

You can develop your own positive affirmations or use King's and Peale's themes to get started in customizing your "daily conversations with self".

DR. BARBARA KING'S 12 AFFIRMATIONS AT A GLANCE

1.	POTENTIAL	• God is the potential that expresses through me.
2.	ANXIETY	• Today is my day to put aside all that worried me yesterday.
3.	LOVE	• I express love on every level, with God, myself, and my fellow human beings.
4.	ORDER	• I am in divine order in my thinking and in my relationships.
5.	FORGIVENESS	• Divine love within me frees me to forgive.
6.	PROTECTION	• I am divinely protected at all times, in all places, and under all circumstances.
7.	PROSPERITY	• Prosperity is my divine birthright.
8.	SELF-ESTEEM	• I deserve the best as a Child of God.
9.	HEALING	• I have faith in God in me to heal my condition.
10.	MIRACLES	• I am a unique, unrepeatable miracle.
11.	SERENITY	• I look inward and upward for peace and happiness.
12.	WEALTH	• I open my consciousness of love for my business, producing overflowing profits.

NORMAN VINCENT PEALE'S "SIX ATTITUDES OF WINNERS" AT A GLANCE

1.	POSITIVE	• No problem is too great to solve.
2.	COURAGEOUS	• I have nothing to fear.
3.	ENTHUSIASTIC	• Life is exciting!
4.	PEACEFUL	• I don't need to worry.
5.	CONFIDENT	• I can change for the better.
6.	EXPECTANT	• I have a future!

_____
_____
_____
_____
_____
_____
_____
_____
_____
_____
_____
_____
_____
_____
_____
_____
_____
_____
_____
_____
_____
_____
_____
_____
_____
_____
_____
_____
_____
_____

TEAMING

"Teaming is about playing to everyone's strengths and holding each member accountable for process and outcomes."

Dr. Quinn Motivates

Creative thinkers and high achievers understand the importance of building functional teams to maximize potential and results. Patrick Lencioni's work on dysfunctional teams provides guidance in helping you get to the root cause of what is causing the current team to be dysfunctional.

PATRICK LENCIONI 'S PERSPECTIVE ON DYSFUNCTIONAL TEAMS	
DYSFUNCTIONS	WHAT NEEDS TO BE WORKED ON
1. ABSENCE OF TRUST	• The fear of being vulnerable with team members prevents the building of trust within the team
2. FEAR OF CONFLICT	• The desire to preserve artificial harmony stifles the occurrence of productive ideological conflict
3. LACK OF COMMITMENT	• The lack of clarity or buy-in prevents team members from making decisions they will stick to
4. AVOIDANCE OF ACCOUNTABILITY	• The need to avoid interpersonal discomfort prevents team members from holding one another accountable
5. INATTENTION TO RESULTS	• The pursuit of individual goals and personal status erodes the focus on collective success

Once you have identified common team dysfunctions, the question becomes "well what does a "functional" team look like? In my work on teams, I have developed the following 25 core elements for building a functional team including: (1) talent; (2) typology; (3) talk; (4) trust; (5) truth; (6) transparency; (7) transactional; (8) transformational; (9) tough; (10) trouble-shooting tools and tactics; (11) excellent work; (12) environmentally appropriate; (13) engagement; (14) empowerment; (15) effective functioning as a family; (16) effective functioning as a business; (17) accountability; (18) aptitude; (19) attitude; (20) active listening; (21) agendas; (22) mission-centered; (23) methods-driven; (24) motivation; and (25) moving managers to leaders.

IT'S TIME TO GO TO WORK: "TEAMING"

"Coming together is a beginning. Keeping together is progress. Working together is success."
Henry Ford

After having studied Patrick Lencioni's work on dysfunctional teams, you learn what you don't want in a team. My work on teams provides insights into what constitutes a functional team poised for high performance. Using both concepts of teaming, rethink your teaming arrangements and agreements. Start with determining the current state of your more intimate personal and professional teams using the assessment model below.

DR. QUINNS ASSESSMENT FOR RECONFIGURING YOUR DREAM TEAM			
	WHO HAS THIS STRENGTH AMONG MY TEAM FROM MY BUILT NETWORK?	WHAT LIFE COACHING ROLE MODELS DO I ACCESS IN THIS AREA?	WHO AND HOW WILL I ADD TO MY TEAM IN THIS AREA?
1. RELATIONSHIPS *(intimate, social, and professional)*			
2. PROFESSIONAL DEVELOPMENT *(career, education, entrepreneurship)*			
3. EMOTIONALLY WHOLE			
4. HEALTH AND WELLNESS			
5. SPIRITUAL			
6. FINANCIAL			

Use my 25 core elements for building a functional team to determine the strengths, challenges, and areas of continued enhancement for the various teams you lead or serve as a member.

DR. QUINN'S 25 CORE ELEMENTS FOR BUILDING A "FUNCTIONAL TEAM"

T (1) Talent * (2) Typology * (3) Talk * (4) Trust * (5) Truth * (6)Transparency * (7) Transactional (8) Transformational * (9) Tough * (10) Trouble-shooting tools and tactics

E (11) Excellent work * (12) Environmentally appropriate * (13) Engagement * (14) Empowerment * (15) Effective functioning as a family * (16) Effective functioning as a business

A (17) Accountability * (18) Aptitude * (19) Attitude * (20) Active listening * (21) Agendas

M (22) Mission-centered * (23) Methods-driven * (24) Motivation * (25) Moving managers to leaders

EMPOWERED FOR LIFE

"Empowerment is a lifestyle and should never be comprised by situations and conditions that present as obstacles. Whatever comes your way remember that you are empowered for life and not easily shaken or broken by circumstances."

Dr. Quinn Motivates

No one inspires us more than Oprah Winfrey in being "empowered for life." My model for being empowered for life emerged as I was reading American author, university lecturer and business writer Janet Lowe's book titled *"Oprah Speaks: Insight form the World's Most Influential Voice."* As I read this publication, I identified themes and patterns about how Oprah embraced an empowered lifestyle that resulted in her beating the odds and reinventing herself several times over throughout her childhood, educational and career endeavors, and business ventures. A summary of salient themes are presented below using an acronym for "EMPOWERED":

"EMPOWERED FOR LIFE" CASE STUDY: OPRAH WINFREY		
E	ENTHUSIASM	• Oprah works with excitement and inspiration in her voice so as to communicate her courage, confidence, and competence.
M	MISSION-CENTERED	• Oprah launches every project with the big picture in mind. She knows the endgame and makes it her personal mission to get the team to the finish line.
P	PURPOSE & PASSION	• Oprah is clear about the purpose of her life, and is passionate about the path to pursue it.
O	OTHER-CENTERED	• Oprah distinguishes between serving and supporting others from pleasing others.
W	WILLPOWER	• Oprah fights through failure with a vengeance no matter the goal.
E	EMOTIONALLY INTELLIGENT	• Oprah is vulnerable and transparent in sharing what's on her heart and mind.
R	RESPONSIBILITY	• Oprah challenges everyone to take full responsibility for every aspect of their own lives. She is a firm believer in information-gathering, partnering effectively, relying upon wise counsel, but views none of these as substitutes for accepting responsibility for one's final choices.
E	EQUITY	• Oprah balances both, sweat and financial equity. She simply values everyone having some skin in the game.
D	DREAM	• Just when we think Oprah has reached her innovative limits, she finds another way to wow us with something new.

IT'S TIME TO GO TO WORK: "EMPOWERED FOR LIFE"

"The process of spotting fear and refusing to obey it is the source of all true empowerment."

Martha Beck

In the space provided below, highlight your action steps for remaining empowered for life using the acronym "EMPOWERED."

DR. QUINN'S "EMPOWERED FOR LIFE" MODEL
FRAME YOUR EMPOWERMENT MAINTENANCE PLAN

E ENTHUSIASM

M MISSION-CENTERED

P PURPOSE & PASSION

O OTHER-CENTERED

W WILLPOWER

E EMOTIONALLY INTELLIGENT

R RESPONSIBILITY

E EQUITY

D DREAM

Walt Disney once said "There is more treasure in books than in all the pirates' loot on treasure island." On that note I must confess that I must be a walking treasure chest because I read right after eating, sleeping, and breathing. Here is a list of 100 books that I read and resulted in the *40 achievement principles* I now use in my life coaching business.

AUTHORS *(in alphabetical order by author's last name)*	TITLE OF BOOK	PRIMARY LIFE COACHING THEME
1. James Allen	As a Man Thinketh	Insight
2. Susan Anderson	The Journey from Abandonment to Healing	Ceasefire
3. Maya Angelou	Phenomenal Women: Four Poems Celebrating Women	Memorable Moments & Milestones
4. Maya Angelou	The Heart of a Woman	Memorable Moments & Milestones
5. Robert Anthony	50 Ideas that Can Change Your Life	Exploration
6. Joanna Barsh and Susie Cranston	How Remarkable Women Lead	Empowered for Life
7. Becky Blalock	DARE: Straight talk on confidence, courage, and career for women in charge	Fortitude
8. Ken Blanchard and Phil Hodges	The Servant Leader: Transforming Your Heart, Head, Hands, and Habits	Radical Results
9. Rick Brinkman & Rick Kirschner	Dealing with People You Can't Stand: How to Bring Out the Best in People at their Worse	New Deal
10. Rovenia M. Brock	Dr. Ro's Ten Secrets to Livin' Healthy	Mirror Moment
11. Brene' Brown	The Gifts of Imperfection	Vulnerability

AUTHORS (in alphabetical order by author's last name)	TITLE OF BOOK	PRIMARY LIFE COACHING THEME
12. Brene' Brown	Daring Greatly: How the Courage to Be Vulnerable Transforms the Way We Live, Love, Parent, and Lead	Vulnerability
13. Brene' Brown	Rising Strong	Fail Forward
14. Elaine Meryl Brown, Marsha Haygood, and Rhonda Joy McClean	The Little Black Book of Success: Laws of Leadership for Black Women	Success Framework
15. Les Brown	Live Your Dreams	Imagination
16. Richard Carlson	Don't Sweat the Small Stuff at Work	Neutralize the Naysayers
17. Dale Carnegie	How To Win Friends and Influence People	New Deal
18. Dale Carnegie	How to Stop Worrying and Start Living: Time-tested Methods for Conquering Worry	Emotions
19. Clayborne Carson	The Autobiography of Martin Luther King. Jr.	Memorable Moments and Milestones
20. Gary Chapman	Everybody Wins: The Chapman Guide to Solving Conflicts Without Arguing	Ceasefire
21. Gary Chapman	The Five Love Languages	Intimacy
22. Gary R. Collins	You Can Make a Difference: 14 Principles for Influencing Lives	Relationships
23. Grace Cornish	10 Good Choices that Empower Black Women's Lives	Choices
24. Stephen R. Covey	The 7 Habits of Highly Effective People: Powerful Lessons in Personal Change	Emotional Intelligence
25. Stephen R. Covey	Living the 7 Habits" The Courage to Change	Risk
26. Stephen R. Covey	First Things First	Order and Organization Time

Authors (in alphabetical order by author's last name)	Title of Book	Primary Life Coaching Theme
27. Stephen R. Covey	The 8th Habit: From Effectiveness to Greatness	Radical Results
28. Samuel A. Cypert	Believe and Achieve: W. Clement Stones 17 Principles of Success	Radical Results
29. Becky A. Davis	Help Yourself: How to Create a Whole New You, More Income, and a Better Life	Teaming
30. Becky A. Davis	The P Factor: If you want Profits, Productivity, and Promotions, Make Purpose and People a Priority	Purpose & Passion
31. Joe Folkman	Turning Feedback into Change: 31 Principles for Managing Personal Development Through Feedback	Success Framework
32. Henry W. Foster Jr.	Make a Difference	Success Framework
33. George C. Fraser	Race for Success	Success Framework
34. Chris Gardner (with Quincy Troupe)	The Pursuit of HappYness	Purpose and Passion
35. Chris Gardner	Start Where You Are: Life Lessons in Getting from Where you are to where you want to be	Radical Results
36. Quinn M. Gentry	Give it All You Got: Unleashing Your Entrepreneurial Spirit	Purpose and Passion
37. Daniel Goleman	Leadership: The Power of Emotional Intelligence	Emotional Intelligence
38. Gwendolyn Goldsby Grant	The Best Kind of Loving: A Black Woman's Guide to Finding Intimacy	Relationships
39. B. Eugene Griessman	The Achievement Factors: Candid Interviews with some of the most successful people of our time	Success Matrix
40. Carla Harris	Expect to Win: 10 Proven Strategies for Thriving in the	Purpose and Passion

AUTHORS (in alphabetical order by author's last name)	TITLE OF BOOK	PRIMARY LIFE COACHING THEME
	Workplace	Think and Move
41. Christine Harvey	Secrets of the World's Top Sales Performers	Radical Results
42. Steve Harvey	Act Like a Success, Think Like a Success: Discovering Your Gift and the Way to Life's Riches	Think and Move
43. Napoleon Hill	Think and Grow Rich	Think and Move
44. Debrena Jackson-Gandy	Sacred Pampering Principles: An African American Woman's Guide to Self-care and Inner Renewal	Nurture
45. Debrena Jackson-Gandy	All The Joy You can Stand: 101 Sacred Power Principles for Making Joy Real in your Life	Intimacy
46. Milton Katselas	Dreams into Action: Getting What you want	Momentum
47. Barbara Killinger	The Balancing Act: Rediscovering Your Feelings	Addictions
48. Dennis Kimbro	Daily Motivations for African-American Success	Affirmation
49. Dennis Kimbro	Think and Grow Rich: A Black Choice	Think and Move
50. Dennis Kimbro	What Makes the Great Great	Fortitude
51. Patrick Lencioni	The Five Dysfunctions of a Team: A Leadership Fable	Teaming
52. Janet Lowe	Oprah Winfrey Speaks: Insight from the World's Most Influential Voice	Empowered for Life
53. John C. Maxwell	How Successful People Think	Think and Move
54. John C. Maxwell	Fail Forward	Fail Forward
55. John C. Maxwell	The Journey from Success to Significance	Success Matrix
56. John C. Maxwell	Be All You Can Be: A Challenge to Stretch to Your God-Given Potential	Natural and Supernatural Strength

Authors (in alphabetical order by author's last name)	Title of Book	Primary Life Coaching Theme
57. John C. Maxwell	The Winning Attitude: Your Pathway to Personal Success	Self-awareness
58. John C. Maxwell	Success Once Day at a Time	Success Matrix
59. Patricia Russell-McCloud	A is for Attitude: An Alphabet for Living	Options and Opportunities
60. Alan L. McGinnis	Bringing Out the Best in People	Teaming
61. Brandi Mitchell	Look the Part to Get the Role	Mirror Moments
62. Norman Vincent Peale	Six Attitudes for Winners	Affirmations
63. Norman Vincent Peale	The Positive Principle Today	Insight
64. M. Scott Peck	The Road Less Traveled: A New Psychology of Love, Traditional Values, and Spiritual Growth	Relationships
65. David B. Peterson and Mary Dee Hicks	Development First: Strategies for Self-Development	Self-awareness
66. Dan Miguel Ruiz	The Four Agreements: A Practical Guide to Personal Freedom	New Deal Intentionality
67. Ian K. Smith	Extreme Fat Smash Diet	Mirror Moment
68. Judy Smith	Good Self, Bad Self: How to Bounce Back from a Personal Crisis	Openness
69. Susan L. Taylor	Lessons in Living	Lessons in Living
70. Iyanla Vanzant	One Day My Soul Just Opened Up: 40 Days and 40 Nights toward Spiritual Strength and Personal Growth	Self-Awareness
71. Iyanla Vanzant	The Value in the Valley: A Black Women's Guide Through Life's Dilemmas	Reality

AUTHORS (in alphabetical order by author's last name)	TITLE OF BOOK	PRIMARY LIFE COACHING THEME
72. Iyanla Vanzant	Peace from Broken Pieces How to Get Through What You're Going Through	Ceasefire
73. Teneshia Jackson Warner	Profit with Purpose: A Marketer's Guide to Delivering Purpose-driven Campaigns to Multi-cultural Audiences	Purpose and Passion
74. Oprah Winfrey	What I Know for Sure	Memorable Moments and Milestones
75. Gary Zukav	The Seat of the Soul	Intuition Intentionality Relationships Choices

The 25 books on the list below are ones that I have used over the years for daily devotions, prayer and meditation. Collectively they all contribute to the process of confirming one's calling and being courageous enough to live by the principles of a purpose-driven life. By way of a shameless plug I am happy to point out that my own commitment to studying God's Word and using various study aids resulted in another book that makes my list titled "In Pursuit of Purpose: *Biblical Guidance for the Entrepreneurial Journey.*"

AUTHORS *(in alphabetical order by last name)*	TITLE OF BOOK
76. Charles Allen	All things are Possible Through Prayer
77. Kay Arthur	Lord Teach Me to Pray in 28 days
78. Kay Arthur, David and BJ Lawson	How to Make Choices You won't regret
79. Nathan Busenitz	Living a Life of Hope: Staying focused on What Really Matters
80. Ric Engram	Pace Yourself: Daily Devotions for Those Who do Too Much
81. Quinn M. Gentry	In Pursuit of Purpose: Biblical Guidance for the Entrepreneurial Journey
82. Billy Graham	Hope for Each Day: Words of Wisdom and Faith
83. T.D. Jakes	Women Thou Art Loosed!
84. King James Version	The Holy Bible: King James Version
85. Edna G. Jordan	Breath Prayers for African Americans
86. Barbara King	Transform Your Life
87. Victoria Lowe	10 Spiritual Principles of Successful Women: Discovering your Purpose, Vision, and Blessing
88. Erwin W. Lutzer	Winning the Inner War: How to Say No to a Stubborn Habit
89. Stormie Omartian	Lord, I want to be whole: Workbook and Journal
90. Robert Schuller	Living Positively One Day at a Time
91. Thomas E. Trask and Wayd I. Goodall	The Fruit of the Spirit: Becoming the person God Wants You to Be
92. Rick Warren	The Purpose Driven Life: What On Earth Am I Here For?
93. Sheretta West	Order My Steps: Learning to Walk the Path that's Ordered by God
94. Bruce Wilkinson	The Prayer of Jabez: Breaking Through to the

AUTHORS *(in alphabetical order by last name)*	TITLE OF BOOK
	Blessed Life
95. Bruce Wilkinson	The Prayer of Jabez: Devotional
96. Bruce Wilkinson	Secrets of the Vine: Breaking Through to Abundance
97. David Wilkerson	Have You Felt Like Giving Up Lately
98. Marianne Wilson	The Gift of Inner Peace: Inspirational Writings by James Allen
99. H. Norman Wright	Chosen for Blessing: Discover your unsearchable riches in Christ
100. Zondervan	God's Words of Life for Women

Final Notes To Self!

"Your journey, your destiny, and your deepest desires are yours to pursue and that responsibility cannot be shared or transferred."

Now Let's Go!

Dr. Quinn Motivates

Made in the USA
Charleston, SC
30 June 2016